THIS
IS
YUR
TIME

Empowering Today's Financial Advisor

To Bill + Anni
In Friendship

THIS
IS
YOUR
TIME

Empowering Today's Financial Advisor

ALAN PARISSE
AND
DAVID RICHMAN

First Edition

For information:
Flagstaff Publishing
2653 Spruce Street
Boulder, CO 80302
Email: flagstaffpublishing@ix.netcom.com
303-444-8080

Printed in the United States of America

ISBN: 0-9726981-0-8

Contents

Dedication

To Friendship.

To the scores of financial professionals whose lives have touched ours and whose words and thoughts have sparked many of the ideas in this book, and to the authors' mutual admiration and respect over the past two decades. Thank you all.

Introduction

The primary intention of this book is to assist Advisors in becoming ever more valuable resources for their clients. The book is based on the authors' many years of experiencing both the ups and the downs of the financial business. To use the current jargon, we both have "been there, done that," and lived to tell the tale. As a result, there is a good deal of our personal experience underlying the ideas presented – our joys, early arrogance, crushing failures, learned humility, eventual victories and subsequent ups and downs. So, if at times we get a bit preachy we hope you will forgive us. It comes from our passion for passing on lessons hard learned.

After all, we all make blunders. Investors make them and Financial Advisors make them. Investor mistakes generally fall into the areas of investment strategy, selection and timing. Advisors have lapses in judgment, sometimes going about their business in what can later prove to be irrational ways.

Contrary to popular belief, most of these blunders are not failures of the intellect. In both good times and bad, they are usually rooted in a failure to manage emotions. If Financial Advisors are to be effective long term, they must understand and monitor both their own emotions and those of their clients. In addition, Advisors must have the ability to communicate clearly, accounting for emotions but unhampered by them. In other words, sometimes the best way to reach a human's rational mind is to make your appeal below the neck—to the heart and the stomach. In this way, Advisors can guide their clients in making a commitment to and sticking with a rational long-term plan. In the process, Advisors can also grow their business in a sustainable fashion.

Throughout the book we have included especially candid comments in "Gloves Off" sidebars. These sidebars contain comments, ideas, stories and quips. Some are intended to be humorous: others are just plain blunt.

Let's get started.

What In The World Happened?

Chapter One

"May You Live in Interesting Times"
Ancient Chinese Curse

The first few years of the 21ˢᵗ Century brought more than their share of *interesting times.*

After Years of Coasting …

As the 20ᵗʰ Century drew to a close business was booming, the future looked brilliant, 401(k)s were overflowing and there was the illusion of everlasting peace in the world. The boom that began in the 1980s had been so bountiful that many of us not only met our financial and career objectives, we exceeded goals we never dared make. Many believed we had entered another age; one in which the so-called New Economy would be exempted from the ups and downs of the past. Some thought we would be shielded from history itself. Francis Fukuyama, a prominent philosopher, even wrote a book declaring the very "End of History." A lot of us believed so completely in our economy's invincibility that we started coasting emotionally and intellectually but didn't know we were doing it. We had reached the dangerous emotional state called "Good Enough" (discussed later). Metaphorically, we had ridden our bicycles downhill for so long that we concluded we were great athletes.

. . . The Terrain Changed

Suddenly, the boom that could never end screeched to a halt. Dot-commers moved back with their parents; mutual funds started seeing net redemptions; a joke circulated that 401(k)s had become 201(k)s; loyal clients started looking for others to counsel them; and overall Advisor income fell. Then, the unimaginable started happening; terrorism was first, followed by revelations that venerable corporate names could not be trusted, nor could the accountants who audited their books, the regulators who monitored their disclosures, the analysts who evaluated their prospects or the CEO's who ran the show. Trust and confidence eroded.

This extraordinary combination of events ended our easy downhill bike ride. As we hit flat ground and had to start pedaling again, we discovered that we had grown fat and out of shape. Suddenly, we found ourselves heading up a mountain with a strong wind in our face.

As challenging as the curse of *interesting times* can be, such times also bring benefits. They present great opportunities for learning, service and reward. In the longer run, demanding times can prove more of a benefit than a curse.

This Is Your Time

So despite all the challenges, and to a considerable extent because of them, this is your time. It is a time to renew yourself and rededicate yourself to your community, your family and your work. Importantly, it is also a time for you to re-commit to your clients and to enhance the service you pro-vide them. Now is the time to create a platform from which to forge ahead with vigor, passion and resolve.

In a volatile environment the role of the Financial Advi-sor is at its most important and valuable. While popular cul-ture perpetuates the myth that the best win is the easy win, deeper satisfaction comes from making contributions of con-sequence against all odds.

A Marathon, Not A Sprint

Fast, easy wins are the recreational drugs of success. They provide momentary highs but eventually result in trauma.

Examples of early successes who later fail abound. There is the high school hero whose athletic career washes out, leaving him a meter reader for the gas company; the prom queen whose maturity broadens her beam, but not her mind or perspective; the child star who fades from the limelight to drug addiction; the lottery winner who ends up broke again; and the do-it-yourself day trader who went from riding in a limousine in 2000 to driving it in 2002. Achieving satisfac-tion in life is indeed a marathon, not a sprint.

In the long run, those who earn what they get, con-tributing as they receive, rushing forward now and then, falling back here and there, tend to have more fulfilling, com-plete and gratifying lives.

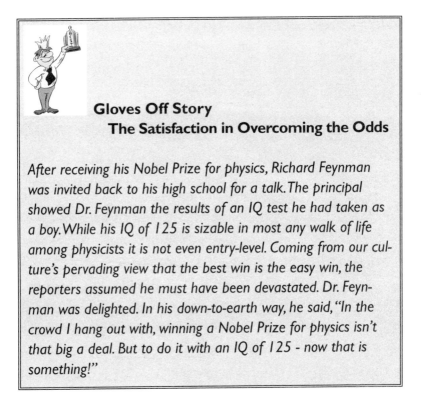

Gloves Off Story
The Satisfaction in Overcoming the Odds

After receiving his Nobel Prize for physics, Richard Feynman was invited back to his high school for a talk. The principal showed Dr. Feynman the results of an IQ test he had taken as a boy. While his IQ of 125 is sizable in most any walk of life among physicists it is not even entry-level. Coming from our culture's pervading view that the best win is the easy win, the reporters assumed he must have been devastated. Dr. Feynman was delighted. In his down-to-earth way, he said, "In the crowd I hang out with, winning a Nobel Prize for physics isn't that big a deal. But to do it with an IQ of 125 - now that is something!"

As an Advisor this is the time to use your efforts, talents and abilities to expand your purpose and reevaluate your mission. It is the time to upgrade your book of clients and make an ever more important contribution to their long-term financial success.

It won't be easy. It takes skill and courage to show an investor the virtue of a rational, long-term, investment plan and then get that investor to stick with the plan through the ups and downs of the market.

Mistakes Made – Damage Done

In the late 1990's, the raging bull market did what bull markets do. It stirred up a dust storm that blinded clients to the wisdom of rational investing and asset allocation. Reason was tossed aside by the thrill of easy money and the anticipation of an exponential rise in portfolios over-weighted in unproven high-tech companies.

At some level, most Advisors knew better. The more experienced had seen down markets before, while less experienced Advisors had at the least read about cycles and bubbles. After all, Charles Mackay's landmark book, *Extraordinary Popular Delusions and the Madness of Crowds*, was published back in 1841. It detailed even earlier investment manias such as the Tulip Mania in Holland in the 1630's, as well as John Law's Mississippi scheme and the South Sea Bubble in the early 1700's. (It is odd. In 1999, those stories seemed ancient. A few years later, however, they seemed very timely.)

Yet, most of those who tried to hold their client's bull market emotions in check eventually succumbed to the stampede of greed. As the market rose Advisors were bombarded by calls from clients gripped by frenzy. "Stop telling me about the risks and all this history nonsense. I have got to get a piece of this market. Everyone around me is getting rich. I'm falling behind. I feel like a fool and it's your fault!"

In the short run, clients had a point. The rational portfolios their advisors had designed were not even keeping up with the broad indices, let alone the selective high-flyers that were being bragged about. Eventually, even seasoned Advisors who knew better found themselves jumping on the gravy train that we now know was headed for a cliff. In the inevitable plunge, clients' financial plans turned into pipe dreams. As a result, many Advisors found their own confidence faltering as their book of clients shrank.

Of course, business and the markets do come back—often sooner than might be supposed. But, memories last and emotional scars remain. Advisors who had made a handsome living cheering on the bull later found themselves dealing with clients who were as concerned and confused as a tourist in a third-world country trying to cross a chaotic intersection to report a stolen wallet. Where should I go? Whom can I trust?

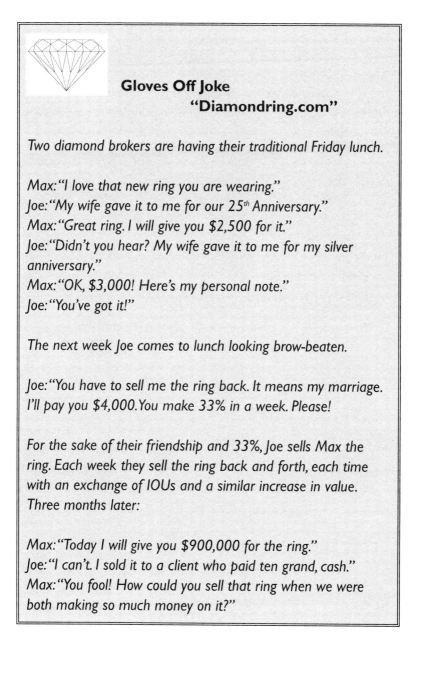

Gloves Off Joke
"Diamondring.com"

Two diamond brokers are having their traditional Friday lunch.

Max: "I love that new ring you are wearing."
Joe: "My wife gave it to me for our 25th Anniversary."
Max: "Great ring. I will give you $2,500 for it."
Joe: "Didn't you hear? My wife gave it to me for my silver anniversary."
Max: "OK, $3,000! Here's my personal note."
Joe: "You've got it!"

The next week Joe comes to lunch looking brow-beaten.

Joe: "You have to sell me the ring back. It means my marriage. I'll pay you $4,000. You make 33% in a week. Please!

For the sake of their friendship and 33%, Joe sells Max the ring. Each week they sell the ring back and forth, each time with an exchange of IOUs and a similar increase in value. Three months later:

Max: "Today I will give you $900,000 for the ring."
Joe: "I can't. I sold it to a client who paid ten grand, cash."
Max: "You fool! How could you sell that ring when we were both making so much money on it?"

Chapter Two

The Erosion of Trust

Trust is the stock in trade of anyone offering advice. The level of trust the person receiving the advice has for the person giving it goes a long way toward determining the value of the advice. Whether it is a lawyer counseling a client, a coach giving pointers to an athlete, or a parent attempting to advise a rebellious teenager, the probability of success is much greater if the advice takes place within the context of trust. Particularly in financial services, a working relationship achieves the desired result when a client has confidence in his or her Advisor's character, ability and truthfulness.

For many clients, a trusting relationship requires more than factual evidence. These clients tend to base their assessment on subjective and emotional grounds. They weigh such things as personality and community reputation heavily, sometimes to the point of transcending the facts. In whatever manner trust is assessed, it is essential. As many Advisors now know all too well, trust takes a long time to establish and only moments to destroy.

A Foundation of Trust

Trust has long been an important aspect of economic life. Even when bartering was the primary method of exchange, this simple, direct exchange of goods was made more efficient when the parties trusted each other. As economics advanced beyond barter to paper money and eventually to electronic transfers, trust became an integral part of the system. In modern times, trillions of dollars are transferred around the world daily, based to some considerable degree on trust. It is the foundation of market economics and the financial services industry. After all, we cannot eat, wear or sleep in paper money or electronic transfers. Bank deposits, securities accounts, life insurance contracts, and annuities are essentially all promises. Consequently, any eroding of the public's trust in our financial institutions can set into motion a stream of critical consequences. The problems Advisors experience in working with their clients is but one representative part.

History Does Not Repeat Itself

Contrary to the popular saying, history does not repeat itself. As Mark Twain pointed out, however, "It rhymes." So we should not be surprised when booms bust or when bears suddenly transform into bulls. Yet, we are surprised and it isn't difficult to understand why. After all, each major swing in our economic fortunes comes for different reasons and often when we least expect it.

Gloves Off Comment
New Contradictions

Oxymorons are a language lover's delight. Often, these contradictions in terms merely underscore the inclination to speak without thinking. Mildly humorous combinations include jumbo shrimp, pretty ugly, good grief and alone together. Other times, however, oxymorons are used to express convictions and beliefs by poking fun. Opinionated examples include rap music, union labor, underpaid CEO, compassionate conservative and thinking liberal. Oxymorons can also be used to expose euphemisms and reveal hidden realities. Friendly fire and minor surgery fall into this category.

Sadly, for the investment business, a few more oxymorons have entered the lexicon: accounting principles, financial reporting and security analyst. More cutting than the new oxymorons, however, is the quip that the behavior of certain accountants, analysts and CFOs has given a whole new meaning to the phrase "bull market."

After more than a decade of boom, the market reversals and economic difficulties experienced at the beginning of the 21st Century would have been sufficiently serious by themselves. Regrettably, other issues accompanied the downturn and exacerbated it. Violence in the world and here at home shook our confidence. In addition, fundamental conflicts of interest that have long existed in the financial community have been revealed to the public. Far worse, the 1990's saw these violations of public trust grow at a rate akin to the initial rise in the stock price of the feistiest dot-coms.

By early in the 21st century regulators, prosecutors and Congress had started scrutinizing public corporations with an intensity not seen in many years. Problems and scandal arose at Enron, Arthur Andersen, Tyco, Rite Aid, Global Crossings, WorldCom, ImClone and others. Celebrity CEOs who were deified in the 90's were demonized in the new millennium.

As if that were not enough, the print media overflowed with revelations questioning the business practices of the Wall Street firms themselves. In May of 2001, *Fortune* magazine ran a cover article under the banner, "Can We Ever Trust Wall Street Again?" The article focused on the activities of Mary Meeker, an analyst at Morgan Stanley who apparently fell in love with the dot-com companies she covered. As the "Queen of the Internet" she continued recommending dot-com stocks to her firm's retail clients long after the stocks' dramatic weaknesses became obvious. Even after her errors were exposed and her title was converted to "Queen of the Internet Bubble," she apparently still did not think she had done anything wrong. Her explanation, said *Fortune*, was that she felt protective toward the phenomenon she helped launch. But what of the investors and Advisors who trusted her?

In the months following the *Fortune* interview, other analysts came under fire in the press. Henry Blodget from Merrill Lynch and Jack Grubman at Salomon Smith Barney were two of the most prominent. And the criticism went beyond the collapse of the stocks they recommended to the conflicts of interest inherent in their role. Rightly so, for it certainly appeared that they were more interested in obtaining investment banking business for their firms and big pay checks for themselves than in fulfilling their role as securities analysts for the benefit of their firms' investors and Advisors.

Mr. Grubman's letter of resignation indicated he too did not think he had done anything wrong. His letter focused on how the "climate of criticism" had made it impossible for him to perform his duties and how "unsubstantiated, negative reports, … caused my family great pain." He said nothing of the pain caused to the families of investors who relied on his advice.

At one point, New York State's attorney general decided that the SEC was dragging its feet. He stepped into the void and seized the headlines. He went after Merrill Lynch and fined it $100 million. He also did his best to humiliate the firm in the press by forcing it to reveal internal emails commenting on stocks the firm was recommending to the public. Some emails said it all too vividly. Referring to Excite at Home, on which the firm had a buy recommendation, one analyst said simply, "Such a piece of crap." In another email, an apparently responsible analyst, Kristen Campbell, wrote to her boss saying, "John and Mary Smith are losing their retirement because we don't want to make the company's CFO mad at us."

All the while the regulators kept hunting and the headlines kept blaring:

BusinessWeek: "How Corrupt is Wall Street?"
The Economist: "The Wickedness of Wall Street."
Fast Company: "Are All Consultants Corrupt?"
The New York Times: "Disinformation on Wall Street."
Forbes: "For Wall Street, the Heat Is On."

On October 14, 2002, an Op-ed article in *The Wall Street Journal* entitled "The Great Wall Street?" by Burton Malkiel, put some numbers to it. He reported that in the late 1990's, buy to sell recommendations reached an astounding ratio of 100-1. The article also discussed a study by Dartmouth and Cornell clearly showing that recommendations by analysts at firms without investment banking departments did much better than those at firms with banking departments. How badly did they do? Brad Barber of the University of California showed that the performance of "strong buy" recommendations during the period he studied underperformed the market by 3.0% while "sell" recommendations outperformed it by 3.8%. There is little wonder why just a few days later Massachusetts accused CSFB of "mocking investors."

What Is an Advisor to Do?

While the leaders of the financial services industry and its regulators address systemic issues and everyone waits for the return of a bull market, what is an Advisor to do?

To start with, there are some things NOT to do.

1. Do not hide from your clients. They need to know you are aware and concerned.
2. Don't assume they are necessarily as familiar with or concerned about the problems and risks as those of us in the business. Don't give them more to worry about, unless they need to know.
3. Don't let your clients "straight line" the ups and downs. In other words, don't let them fall into the trap of extrapolating either a downward trend and a negative press cycle or a gleeful press cycle and booming market indefinitely into the future.

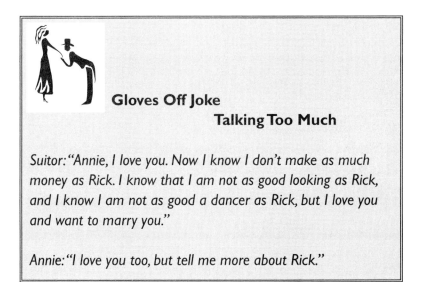

Gloves Off Joke
Talking Too Much

Suitor: "Annie, I love you. Now I know I don't make as much money as Rick. I know that I am not as good looking as Rick, and I know I am not as good a dancer as Rick, but I love you and want to marry you."

Annie: "I love you too, but tell me more about Rick."

When a Tiger Enters the Temple ...

When times get tough, it is much better to "step into" a problem than to back away from it or pretend it isn't there. As the ancient Asian saying goes: "When a tiger enters the temple, include it in the ceremony." In other words, don't avoid the issue. Use it to make your point.

First, listen to your clients and let them vent: hear and understand their concerns. Then, to show your understanding of both the facts and their feelings, include their concerns in your response. For example, when a client says, "With all those conflicts of interest, I will NEVER trust investment advice again. I am going to go it alone," don't apologize and launch into a detailed explanation. Rather, include their concerns in the ceremony. Try saying, "I understand how you can feel that way. ... Frankly, however, that is actually the reason you ought to be working with me. "

So far so good, but what should you say after the client asks why? To some extent, the answer is a function of the way you as the Advisor and your firm are positioned. If an Advisor is with an independent financial planning firm or an insurance-based organization, he or she might stress the fact that the firm does not have an investment banking function and is free of the conflicts of interest that plague both Wall Street and the large professional services firms.

But What if My Firm Is the One in the News?

Try this.

Advisor: "It is at times like these that you need caring, professional advice more than ever. Please understand that you are not engaging a firm or an industry. You are engaging me. It is my job to protect you from whatever conflicts of interest are out there. Let me show you how we can work together. …"

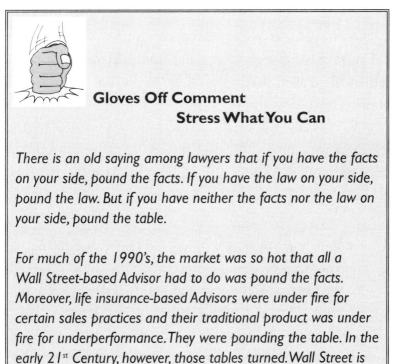

**Gloves Off Comment
Stress What You Can**

There is an old saying among lawyers that if you have the facts on your side, pound the facts. If you have the law on your side, pound the law. But if you have neither the facts nor the law on your side, pound the table.

For much of the 1990's, the market was so hot that all a Wall Street-based Advisor had to do was pound the facts. Moreover, life insurance-based Advisors were under fire for certain sales practices and their traditional product was under fire for underperformance. They were pounding the table. In the early 21st Century, however, those tables turned. Wall Street is taking the heat while insurance agents can pound the facts. The key is to stress the advantages that you have.

Reestablishing Credibility

That's fine, but what if the Advisor shares a degree of responsibility for the client's problems? After all, credibility is a lot easier to lose than gain. How can an Advisor reestablish credibility when he or she did not advise a client to rebalance at the top of a bull market or the depths of a bear market?

The first step is to reestablish your own credibility with yourself. This subject is discussed in depth in the chapter entitled "Advisor – Heal Thyself". For now, here are two quick ideas.

Once again, step into the problem. Don't avoid your clients by putting your head in the sand and hoping the problems will go away. Rather, politely present the client with a choice.

"Mr. and Ms. Client, for you to achieve your goals in the long run we must work together and that means we have to trust each other. I know ____ (choose the appropriate comment below).

1. Your portfolio has suffered and that concerns me considerably, or
2. We have missed the upturn and that distresses me.

In fact, in a very real sense, I have experienced your pain in my own account. For us to move forward, however, requires that we learn from what has happened and then let it go so we can reestablish a working trust. To do that, you have to make a decision about me.

Either you see me as:
- an intelligent person,
- with integrity,
- who made some errors in judgment, and
- learned from those miscalculations.

Or you see me as:
- a fool, or
- a crook.

If the latter is the case, then all I can do is offer my help in finding someone else to handle your account. If, however, you can accept that I am an honest and intelligent person who has learned some difficult lessons, then we can start building for the future. The choice is yours."

Somewhere along the line, you might also point out that if they choose someone new chances are high that their new Advisor will either be:

- A rookie who has not made any errors … yet, or
- An experienced Advisor who likely made his or her blunders with someone else's account.

You might also mention that you have been picking up a number of new accounts lost by other Advisors and while you appreciate the new business, you would rather move to a higher level of trust with your established clients. After all, broken bones often heal strongest at the place where they fractured.

Will you lose some clients this way? Probably. But you will have cleared the air and started to reestablish your credibility with the rest.

Get Your Dignity Back: Fire a Client

Even in the best of times, most Advisors cling to one or two clients who have them thinking that "Life is too short for this." Often, those clients don't produce much income and even if they do, they sap more in energy, heart and soul.

It is understandable that an Advisor might feel a personal obligation to certain clients. For example, a client who was there in the early days or one who is dealing with a personal tragedy. There are times when charity work is appropriate. No doubt it is good for the soul, but only if it is kept within bounds and is appreciated by the recipients.

Yet, even where human concern plays no part, Advisors hang on. The reason may be that most Advisors started on their metaphorical knees looking for their first few clients. The very idea of giving one up is an anathema.

Whatever the reason, you probably have at least one or two clients you would rather not have.

Here's a way to do yourself a favor, get your dignity back and start reestablishing your credibility all at the same time.

Pick a client or two, call them up and say something like this: "Mr. Smith, I have been looking over the service I provide my clients. I have been thinking that I am not the best person to serve your needs. What I would like to do is help you find another Advisor that might be more in sync with your goals and objectives." Then see what happens. Perhaps you will get an opportunity to train the client. More likely, they will go somewhere else. In either event, you get your dignity back and can start upgrading your book to include more desirable clients. Now, if you can just keep the rest of your clients from watching television. . . .

Gloves Off Story
Loose Lips Don't Necessarily
Sink Ships

It was just a routine test, but it showed a virulent cancer and the doctors operated immediately. Lying in post-op, the Advisor got a demanding call from his biggest client, an options trader who represented fully 80% of the Advisor's income. The client's only question was, "Who is watching my account?" With his tongue loosened by the residual anesthesia, the Advisor told the client what he thought of him and his question. The next day the Advisor tried to save the account, but it was too late.

Two years later the Advisor had fully recovered from the cancer and was earning more than ever. "That client was 80% of my income but 200% of my time, energy, dignity and spirit. At times, I think the cancer was God's way of telling me to get that client out of my life and assume control of my business. And, oh yes, within a year of leaving me, the client went bankrupt."

Chapter Three

The Media Piles On

In the 1970's film, *Network*, Peter Finch won an Academy Award as a combative newscaster who was "mad as hell and ... not going to take it anymore." It is a rare Advisor who hasn't had a similar thought while watching the manner in which financial news is often presented to the investing public.

No doubt the media has a powerful societal influence on investor emotions, one that is often troublesome for an Advisor to counteract. Whether intended or not the media confuses the investing public by barraging them with data or "noise" in the guise of meaningful investment information.

It is important to recognize, however, that freedom of the press and the free flow of information are cornerstones of a free society and our market economy. While a constant barrage of investment hype is annoying and can be detrimental, it is a lot better than a closed system rife with insider secrets. Clearly the solution is not to censor the financial media. Rather we should understand what they are and use the information they present appropriately.

Advisors can use the media to their advantage by offering meaningful content with little or no noise. To do that, it is important to think through the media's role and shortcomings.

Gloves Off Comment
Let's Be Fair

There is a tendency in our culture to blame the media, especially television, for everything from obesity to the perceived rise in immorality and violence. While it seems reasonable to conclude that the media bears some responsibility for the problems on which it reports, it is down right silly to blame television for all of society's ills or the market's problems.

Just as Financial Advisors overcome the inherent conflicts of interest in their role and the bad behavior of some in the business, there are television, radio and print commentators who do an excellent job overcoming their mediums' biases and who work hard to serve their audiences' best interests.

That said, there is little doubt that the financial media can create a barrier to rational investing and often does a disservice to the investing public. So, here we go. ...

It's the Ratings, Stupid

Many of your clients still place newscasts on a pedestal. It is understandable. It wasn't that long ago that network owners felt a moral obligation to provide the public with the news they needed to know. Profit was secondary. But the days when CBS anchor Walter Cronkite was the most trusted person in America are gone. Now, the networks and much of the print media are publicly traded companies focused on income, expenses and earnings per share.

To keep their income up, they must focus on ratings or circulation. To get ratings, management seems to have decided that it must give viewers what they appear to want. As a result, both the stories selected and the ways in which they are presented are often skewed. Emphasis is placed on the dramatic and exciting, often at the expense of accuracy, completeness and usefulness. Shows and stories are selected and presented so that they will be interesting to the public, even if they are not in the public's interest.

Think about it. Which is cheaper to produce and more exciting to watch? A show that:

- Provides meaningful discussions of financial planning issues, in-depth studies of historical and future trends and careful analysis of individual issues, or
- Treats the markets like a horse race, reporting on daily movements, and trying to assign cause and effect to them.

Years ago, Roger Ailes put it well when he said that television is not an entertainment medium or a news medium, "It is an advertising medium." Put another way, advertisers are the primary audience.

Playing to Fear and Greed

To create interest and drama, many financial news shows use the oldest investment sales trick in the book. In a bull market, they glorify investor greed. In a bear market, they feed investor fears. In other words, they use your clients' emotions as kindling for their ratings and advertising fires.

Let Us Entertain You

Despite significant efforts to make it an interactive tool, television remains primarily an entertainment vehicle. As David Poltrack, the head of research at CBS put it, "TV is something you do when you don't want to do anything." In the extended bull market of the 1990's, viewers were indeed entertained by reports of a rising market and the related increases in their investment portfolios. In a bear market, however, news of a market drifting down is both boring and depressing. As a result, ratings suffer.

A Bicycle Accident Is Not WWIII

One solution to the ratings challenge is sensationalism. Clients need to understand that volatility and scandal are to financial news programs what car crashes are to NASCAR and fistfights are to hockey.

A century ago, George Bernard Shaw succinctly commented on the newspapers of his time, saying that the media has little motivation to distinguish between a bicycle accident and the collapse of civilization. If that sounds far-fetched, notice the similarity between the amount of airtime and the grave tone of reporting the nightly news gives to a grisly murder and the home team's loss of the big game. They even use similar descriptive words for both: tragic, sudden, shocking, disastrous, hapless, unfortunate and the like.

Motion Is Not Movement

The media often misrepresents what is merely meaningless motion as though it's meaningful, even momentous, movement. It tends to aggregate and then aggrandize what are in fact isolated incidents to the point where they appear to be tenacious trends. And when there are clear trends they are presented as permanent destiny. So, even when the underlying facts are correct, the misimpression created can easily lead investors and Advisors astray.

The Bell Doesn't Ring

Logic tells us that when markets are unstable and investors are running scared a savvy investor should stockpile cash and wait for the "bell to ring", indicating that the markets have settled down and it's safe to put their money to work again. Yet, the bell never rings in time, and even the relentless round of

24-hour TV news won't make that strategy work. While clearly there are times when one is better off on the sidelines, few investors can even begin to accurately predict when the downturn will end and markets will turn up. As a result, sideline sitters usually remain there too long. Many wait to join the next boom after it has peaked and thereby set themselves up to suffer another setback.

Information Overload

In large part, the "investment advice" that financial media pundits pound your clients with isn't investment advice at all. It is, instead, trading information posing as investment advice. Even as trading information, it is often of limited value as it usually comes too late.

Content aside, the very glut of financial news causes immeasurable wear and tear on the typical client. Few investors really need to know how the market is doing minute-by-minute, hour-by-hour, or even day-by-day. It's just not meaningful information for investors with long-term investment needs and plans. Yet, many of them think it is and that often causes those investors to behave in a manner that is at odds with their long-term needs and their best interests.

True Believers Smelling Their Own Perfume

To be fair, the vast majority of financial journalists sincerely want to protect and inform investors. Most even believe they are achieving those ends. That is part of the problem. The context out of which they are operating is not conducive to meeting their ends. As one commentator on the press put it, "You people create a myth and then you believe it." True believers are usually much more effective at selling their myths than are sly cynics. That is especially true when fame and fortune have them smelling their own perfume and falling in love.

An Advisor Can Turn the Volume Down

If you have any doubts that turmoil sells airtime try to imagine one of the financial talking heads saying, "There really isn't much going on in the financial world today. Risk is low and earnings are stable. Why don't you watch a movie or go play with your kids?" You certainly won't hear that on television,

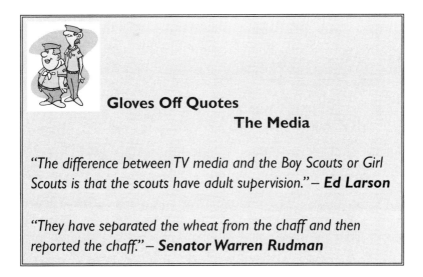

Gloves Off Quotes
The Media

"The difference between TV media and the Boy Scouts or Girl Scouts is that the scouts have adult supervision." – **Ed Larson**

"They have separated the wheat from the chaff and then reported the chaff." – **Senator Warren Rudman**

but as an Advisor, you have the power to say exactly that to your clients. You can help them turn down the volume, ignore the hubbub and concentrate on what's really going on.

Turning the volume down for clients usually starts with the Advisor turning it down for himself or herself. That takes doing the introspective work, feeling the pain after a downturn, avoiding arrogance in an upturn, learning the lessons in between, reestablishing one's own credibility and then moving on.

Moving On

Chapter Four

What To Do Now

So that's the history. But it is only the history. The pertinent question is: "What to do now?" Here are some ideas.

Answer the Wake-Up Call

Wake-up calls are often personal: a serious illness, the loss of a loved one, a car accident. Occasionally they affect a wider group: a community, a country or the world. In either case, these pattern interruptions can be shocking and painful. They jolt us, removing us from our comfort zone and the certainty of the familiar.

Pattern interruptions are not entirely negative, however. In fact, some of them are positive—winning the lottery, for example. In any case, pattern interruptions shake us out of our norm. In so doing, they shift us out of automatic, open us to new ideas and encourage us to reassess our priorities. A wake-up call can ignite our creativity and renew our passion for our work and our lives. Whether they originally seem good or bad, pattern interruptions often present extraordinary long-term benefits, if one seizes them.

Pause, Please!

As soon as possible after a pattern interruption hit the pause button and get ready to absorb new information and gain fresh insight. When extraordinary events occur too many of us simply shut down. We cling to previously held beliefs. For example, after September 11, 2001, many people just reinforced their old beliefs. If they were hawks on September 10th, they reached for their guns on September 12th. If they were doves before the attacks, they sang, *Give Peace a Chance* afterwards. For the religious, it was a time to come to God. For the godless, it was evidence that religion is evil. Only a few seemed to use the pattern interruption to examine their attitudes and positions. Yet, whether the pattern interruption is a widespread tragedy, the loss of a loved one, a personal health challenge or simply missing a market turn, there is value in pausing and thinking it out.

Think Long Term

Short-term issues understandably demand our attention. It is our ability to keep our eye on long-term trends and relationships that decides our future.

In a sound-bite culture there is a tendency to be short-term oriented and lose all perspective. At times, the behavior of both investors and Advisors could be likened to that of a vegetable gardener who is so concerned about how her carrots are doing that she digs them up every day to examine the roots. Yet, she wonders why she gets wilted carrots. Carrots and investments need time and care to grow and flourish.

Set your sights on the long term and then plan for it and work toward it.

Notice the Long-Term Truth

Here is the most important lesson learned during our combined fifty years in the investment business—a truth that many of us forgot during the long bull market of the 1990's and again forgot during the bear market that followed.

This is profound …

Things go up
And
Things go down
And
Then they go up again
And
Then they go down again.

Doesn't sound profound, does it? Perhaps that is why so many of us miss it. There is more …

When things are going up,
The smartest people in the world

Use the most sophisticated computer models
To tell us things will continue to go up roughly,
approximately FOREVER!
When things are going down,
We are told they will continue to go down until they die,
But that is rarely what happens.
Things go up.
Then they go down.
Then they go up again!

In short, cycles rule. Permanent changes do occur, but they are very rare. Yellow lights should come on any time we hear, "Things are really different this time," "This is a New Economy," "A New World Order," "A Permanent Peace." In global politics, investments and life, most of the time we are dealing with cycles.

Many years ago, a Hollywood agent described the cycle of stardom using as an example one of the beautiful leading ladies of the time.

Stage 1: Who is Rita Hayworth?
Stage 2: How about Rita Hayworth?
Stage 3: Let's get Rita Hayworth.
Stage 4: We will only do it if we can get Rita Hayworth.
Stage 5. Get me a Rita Hayworth type.
Stage 6: Get me a young Rita Hayworth.

Stage 7: Whatever happened to Rita Hayworth?
Stage 8: Who is Rita Hayworth?

Don't Distort the Long-Term Whole for a Short-Term Advantage

Don't let short-term efforts to protect yourself ruin your long-term game plan.

Investors do this all the time. They have long-term needs and short-term emotions. They often confuse macro portfolio issues with micro investment issues. Don't let short-term events take them off their game plan ... or you off yours.

Don't Try to Recreate Past Success

When booms bust, many want things to go back to "normal" and try to recreate the past. It rarely works. Ask the parents of hormonally tortured 16 year olds if it works to treat them as the delightful 12 year olds they once were. That was then, this is now. The future is in front of us. Stay the course. Given time, even teenagers have a way of suddenly transforming into sentient young adults.

In prosperous times, it is best not to dwell on past success. In tough times it is critical to focus on the future. When mistakes have been made, take the hit, learn the lessons and then move forward.

Investors often get in trouble when they say, "I just want to get even and then …" So do Advisors. The past is done.

Similarly, in a bull market many clients and Advisors try to catch up to the neighbors' real or imagined success. Catching up rarely works and is very risky.

Create anew from where you are. If moving forward requires you to take a few steps back it is usually best to do it without delay. So, realistically assess your situation, delineate your intentions, lay your plans and start moving toward new successes.

Good News / Bad News

Even in the worst of times, keep in mind that there is almost always good news hidden in bad and opportunity buried in tragedy. That is not to say that the good necessarily outweighs the bad. Clearly, it might not. The more tragic the news, however, the more important it is to identify and cultivate whatever good can come out of it personally, for our community or society at large. The terrorist attacks in September 2001 were tragic. Yet, they also brought an increased sense of community, a reordering of priorities and an awakening of patriotism. More common tragedies of nature, such as earthquakes and hurricanes, often have similar positive effects.

For example, take John Walsh. He found good in the most tragic of circumstances. As a very successful young real estate developer, he and his family enjoyed the good life. He thought his family was exempt from the horrible crimes one reads about in the newspaper. Then his son was abducted and murdered. Realizing, for the first time, that violent crime can happen to even the sheltered affluent, he started the television show, *America's MostWanted*. Over the years his show has established an impressive track record of finding violent criminals. Given the choice, it seems certain that Mr. Walsh would drop the show and take his son back. For him, the good he has created will never outweigh the bad that was done to his family. Yet, he has created a lot of good. The same holds true for Candy Lightner, one of the founders of Mothers Against Drunk Driving. As with Mr. Walsh's television show, MADD was created out of tragedy. A drunk driver killed Ms. Lightner's daughter.

So, when you read the daily newspaper or watch TV news, remember that there is good news for someone buried in the bad news reported by the media. After all, snow storms are bad, but not for skiers; floods are bad, but not for pump manufacturers; hailstorms are bad, but not for auto body shops; earthquakes are bad, but not for home-repair companies, recessions are bad, but not for bankruptcy lawyers; and stock market crashes are bad, but not for short-sellers.

On a personal level, sometimes "bad" turns into "good." When going through a divorce almost everyone says it's bad. Years later, however, many come to believe that the split was a good thing.

When Bill Gates dropped out of Harvard chances are his

parents thought it was bad. Had he waited to graduate the opportunity for him to build Microsoft into the dominant company it is would have passed.

Even some of the worst personal news can be an opportunity for growth. When cyclist Lance Armstrong first learned of his advanced testicular cancer it would have been impossible to convince him that he would one day look back on this painful, nearly fatal experience as a positive. But he does. Since then he has won the Tour de France time and again.

And what of the anthrax threat? Clearly it was bad and could get worse. Yet, even here there is the potential for good. The systems that the U.S. and other countries established to cope with bio-terrorism are expected to help considerably in dealing with the fast-spreading West Nile virus.

So, look for the good news buried in the bad, expand on it and move on.

Reviewing the Situation

Since the beginning of the new millennium, there has been a series of pattern interruptions. As an Advisor, it is a time to use fresh eyes to:

- Review what has happened in the economy, the markets and the world.
- Acknowledge the effects on you and your clients.
- Create a new version of your long-term mission and short-term goals.

- Rededicate yourself to your family, your community and your clients.
- Upgrade your clientele and refocus your efforts where you can do the most good.
- Renew yourself emotionally and physically.

It is important for Advisors to continually adjust their attitudes. That way they can provide their clients with the balanced perspective necessary for long-term success. In both good times and bad, Advisors must assess the situation and provide their clients with confidence, conviction and resolve.

Chapter Five

Needed: Your Confidence, Conviction and Resolve

Providing financial advice and establishing successful client relationships require knowledge, skill and ability. The most important determinants of success lie in the Advisor's:

- *Enthusiasm* about the service he or she provides,
- *Certainty* of his or her ability to provide that service, and
- *Commitment* to his or her clients.

In any market condition an Advisor's conviction and resolve are critical.

Stop Making Problems Worse

When mistakes are made our reactions often prove more damaging than the problems themselves. Administrators become so concerned about their jobs that they stop doing them. Executives and managers worry so much about budgets that they avoid taking sensible risks or making critical investments. Advisors get frozen in the headlights; they refrain from making calls, meeting clients and taking definitive positions.

In all of the above cases there are two sets of problems:

- Real external issues with which they must deal, and
- Their internal reactions to those external problems.

Try this exercise. Visualize a platform with a non-slip surface built six inches above the ground. Make the platform three feet wide and 500-feet long. Assuming a person is able-bodied and steps lively, he or she should be able to walk the length in a few minutes with very little chance of falling. Next, imagine the same platform at 5,000 feet above the ground. How long would it take to walk the length now and what would be the chance of falling? It would almost certainly take a lot longer and, even assuming a cloudless day with no wind, the likelihood of falling would go up dramatically. But the task is the same, so why all the difficulty?

The quick answer is the fear generated by our assessment of the risk. Think about it. Perched high in the air, we correctly determine that there are serious consequences to a misstep. Our strategy for dealing with this very real risk is to become fearful. As a result, our bodies tense, our speed slows and our chances of falling go way up. If we could just remain calm and focus on the task at hand, i.e., walking the length of the platform, without adding fear to the problem, we

Gloves Off Story
Making Matters Worse

At the depths of a down market, a young Advisor bemoaned his fate. "I got into the business at a bad time." He failed to understand that unsettled markets mean restless investors ready to hear a new voice and a fresh perspective. As markets settle down, clients become comfortable and moving them is far more difficult. To succeed long term, our young Advisor must identify and take advantage of such windows of opportunity.

Across the hall, a senior Advisor sat looking at the panoramic view from the window of her elegant corner office. Frustrated, she was thinking, "I was right for eleven years. From the time I entered the business, almost everything I told my clients worked. I got so full of myself that I was telling people how to raise their children. I don't have any children! Then the market broke. ... The other day, a friend from out of town asked me to suggest a place for dinner and I found myself saying, 'That depends on what you like.' If I won't even recommend a restaurant, how can I call my clients and tell them what to do with their money? I've lost my touch. I have no confidence, and I don't seem to be able to advise my clients without it."

could walk across this higher platform just as easily as the lower with as little likelihood of falling.

In the mountainous terrain of financial advice the problems we make are often worse than the problems we have.

Even Media Mania Can Work to Your Advantage

Clearly, media mania is a problem for investors and a nuisance to most Advisors. Conversely, the media can actually be an Advisor's ally. As investors tire of the media barrage, a relationship with a trusted Advisor becomes all the more attractive. Not only will the Advisor give more personally tailored advice, he or she can offer an eloquent island of calm in the noisy sea.

Thought Flooding

The investing public is so overloaded with investment news that many are suffering from a psychological condition known in lay terms as "thought flooding." When functioning normally, the human mind gets its thoughts one at a time in rapid, sequential order. People suffering from thought flooding, however, get their thoughts in bunches.

With so much information and misinformation coming their way, people just cannot sort or process it all. Imagine trying to cross a busy street in this condition. A horn honks and you get thirty thoughts all at once. What do you do? Most of us would either freeze or spin around in circles. Isn't that what investors often do? A good Advisor will help clients avoid the pitfalls and perils that thought flooding can create by sorting through the melee and focusing the investor's attention on the important information.

Now, it is all the more important for you to help set your clients straight and show them how to steer a steady course through the 24/7 information torrent. That takes confidence and courage.

Take a Stand

For years, Advisors have been told to "ask for the order." While asking for the order is a quantum leap from "explaining and waiting," it is no longer sufficient. This is especially true due to the way Advisors tend to ask. Upon completing a presentation, Advisors have been known to sit back and say, "Well, what do you think?" Imagine asking this of clients who are already thought flooded about investing. Clients and prospects need your services more than they ever have, but they don't need you to ask any more. They need you to tell them what to do.

When dealing with affluent investors it is especially important to take a stand, even when this might go against the grain of the client. It does clients no good for you to stroke their egos by agreeing with everything they say. Clients must hear and believe your convictions.

Conventional wisdom might dictate that you should appease a client and avoid being too forceful in your advice.

After all, you want to keep the account. Yet, it does not help clients to hire a yes-person any more than it would for over-weight smokers to hire a doctor who tells them, puff away and eat up. First, win your clients' trust and be worthy of it. Once you know their dreams and fears you can become the caring, competent captain of the ship. In other words, you will be able to advise your clients, in no uncertain terms, of the proper course of action. They will listen to you, they will respect you, they will refer friends to you . . . or . . . they will go away. You will have built a book of clients on your terms, not on theirs, and they will be the biggest beneficiaries.

Your Fees

In good times advisory fees are usually not a major issue. When clients are making 20% or more per annum a 1% or 2% advisory fee seems a small price to pay. Logically and emotionally the fee seems fair. Logically, the Advisor certainly seems to be doing the job and there is plenty of room for the fee. More-over, the effective fee on bank deposits is so much higher. After all, banks take your money and lend it out at credit-card rates, paying you a very small fraction of it. Emotionally, clients don't usually have much of a problem paying fees when times are good. Their typical reaction could be likened to that of a casino gambler. Nonsensical as it is, most gamblers feel differently about losing money they just won than they do about losing money they brought with them. In this case, investors seem to see themselves as paying with the house's money.

Gloves Off Presentation Idea
Get Those Charts Out

Every Advisor has seen the charts that show the devastating impact that timing the markets has on most investors' long-term performance. It's time to dust those charts off and start using them again. Never assume that what is second nature to you is known to your client or prospect. Understand that your awareness of historical trends shows clients that you have a long-term perspective. It will boost clients' confidence that your advice is far more relevant than watching a play-by-play of the market's every move.

When the market is humming along and there is a fee objection, it is relatively easy for a skilled communicator to overcome it. The Advisor simply shows clients the many services and resources that will be made available to them. If the client objects, the tried-and-true comeback is, "The important question for you isn't what I make, it is what you make." That usually works … but only in good times.

In difficult times, advisory fees loom large. That is especially true when clients are losing money or barely breaking even. It is a double whammy. Not only do clients see themselves as paying for advice with their own money, they question whether the

Advisor is doing the job. One of the most emotionally difficult situations is when the client has a small profit before fees and the fees take the return into negative territory. All of a sudden it's the only thing they want to talk about.

Prospects Today Are Willing to Pay for Solid Advice

Despite these concerns, in tough times clients are willing to pay for advice. These investors do not want just any advice. They want committed advice from Advisors who know how to communicate the value of their services, who are willing to take a stand and who are willing to tell their clients what in the world to do.

A bear market is not the time to be wishy-washy or to patronize clients with happy talk. Happy talk works when the bull is raging. In difficult times, however, it is vitally important that you tell your clients what you think and, when appropriate, what they should do. After all, your clients are not only paying you for your advice but also for your confidence. It is right that you give it to them.

Advisors must be definitive, take stands, look to the future, see opportunities in difficulty, think clearly and rationally, sort out issues, calm their clients' emotions with intelligent information and move ever forward.

In a declining market, all of that is easier said than done. In the absence of perceived value, clients will drill you on the fees. You should see the fee objection as an open door to re-

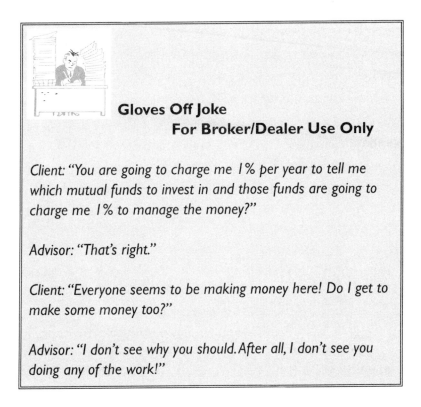

Gloves Off Joke
For Broker/Dealer Use Only

Client: "You are going to charge me 1% per year to tell me which mutual funds to invest in and those funds are going to charge me 1% to manage the money?"

Advisor: "That's right."

Client: "Everyone seems to be making money here! Do I get to make some money too?"

Advisor: "I don't see why you should. After all, I don't see you doing any of the work!"

assert your value proposition. If you have communicated how good you are and how valuable your process is to clients, fees should not become a deal killer.

Always make sure that you understand the context of the fee objection. If the client says, "Your fee seems high," you might ask, "Compared to what?" If a separate account solution you are proposing seems high compared to a managed mutual fund product, be certain the client knows the difference between "all inclusive" fees and advisory fees, which do not include the internal costs to manage the mutual funds and the funds' transaction costs. If the client is comparing the mutual fund costs you are proposing to his or her having to continue picking individual stocks alone, play with any analogy that fits the moment. If someone down the street is offering advice cheaper than you are, consider suggesting that fees are the last thing he or she should focus on. "If you go to a restaurant where the food isn't so good but the price is right, are you going back?"

Don't apologize to your clients and prospects about your

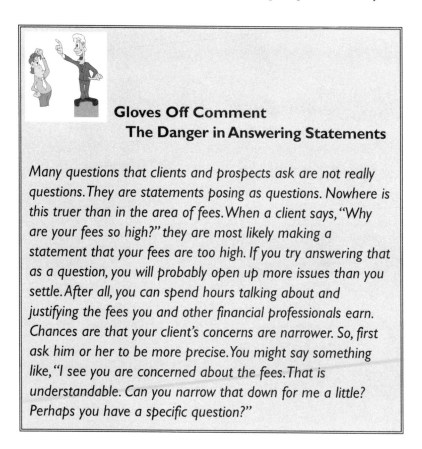

Gloves Off Comment
The Danger in Answering Statements

Many questions that clients and prospects ask are not really questions. They are statements posing as questions. Nowhere is this truer than in the area of fees. When a client says, "Why are your fees so high?" they are most likely making a statement that your fees are too high. If you try answering that as a question, you will probably open up more issues than you settle. After all, you can spend hours talking about and justifying the fees you and other financial professionals earn. Chances are that your client's concerns are narrower. So, first ask him or her to be more precise. You might say something like, "I see you are concerned about the fees. That is understandable. Can you narrow that down for me a little? Perhaps you have a specific question?"

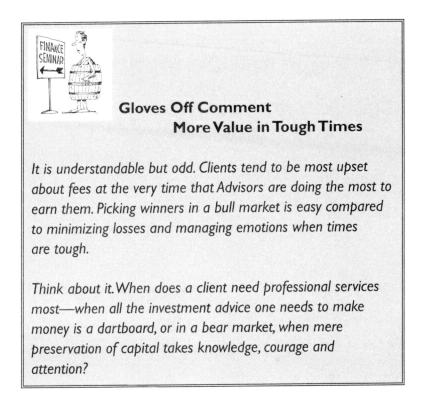

Gloves Off Comment
More Value in Tough Times

It is understandable but odd. Clients tend to be most upset about fees at the very time that Advisors are doing the most to earn them. Picking winners in a bull market is easy compared to minimizing losses and managing emotions when times are tough.

Think about it. When does a client need professional services most—when all the investment advice one needs to make money is a dartboard, or in a bear market, when mere preservation of capital takes knowledge, courage and attention?

fees. Rather, stand tall while you tell them what you do for them and that you are worth every penny. If you believe it, say it. If you don't, then enhance the service you provide so that you do.

Enhancing service requires that you be in tiptop shape, especially emotionally and physically. After all, if the doctor is sick, the patients are in trouble.

Chapter Six

Advisor: Heal Thyself

The first job of a dedicated physician is to remain sufficiently healthy both emotionally and physically to serve his or her patients well. In spite of that, from the very beginning of a would-be doctor's course of study, the stress is on. The pressure to perform is so intense that the physician's physical and psychological health is often ignored. And as for diet, recent studies have shown that the typical medical resident devours a diet far less healthy than the pizza and pop that permeate the offices of Silicon Valley, technology companies. Both doctors and patients suffer due to this woeful lapse from medical education to practice.

Do not let your clients suffer from a similar self-neglect. Keep in mind that a critical part of an Advisor's job is to remain healthy; financially, physically and, most importantly, emotionally.

Examine Your Attitude

Ask yourself the tough questions you ask your clients to answer. Check your own view of the future. And be willing to make changes in the way you live and do business so that you can thrive in whatever new environment you find yourself.

Good Enough Isn't

When times are good for an extended period, individuals and organizations are gradually lulled into that emotional state we call *Good Enough*. This is when we say, "Things are fine. Clients are in good shape. We have surpassed our goals, analysts tell us we're in a New Economy, and the market can go up indefinitely."

This emotional lassitude not only exposes you and your clients to investment risk it also creates a business and personal risk for the Advisor. Among other things, it puts a lid on the Advisor's growth. When things are the way we want them—when they are *Good Enough*—there is a strong tendency to try to hold them in place, to put them in a container. It rarely works.

Good Enough Can Destroy Optimism

Counterintuitive as it may seem, when *Good Enough* creeps up on us and takes over, it is an indication that we have begun to lose our fundamental optimism. By deciding the status quo is as good as it needs to be, we are also saying it cannot get any better. Our view of the future shifts: progress is no longer needed and perhaps not even a possibility.

Good Enough can be very comfortable in the short term.

The ride is smooth and temporarily we have no worries. The problem is that we have put a self-imposed lid on our imagination, our performance and our satisfaction. We have built a fence around ourselves and locked the gate.

We should not be surprised then to find that this emotional state soon proves unsatisfying. More seriously, unless checked, our unconscious pessimism will eventually debilitate us.

By definition, life is movement and change. If we are alive, we are either moving forward or backward. By locking us in place, *Good Enough* sets us up to fail.

An Exception: A Conscious Choice

The desire to hold a *Good Enough* career in place makes sense when it is a conscious choice. For example, a father who decides to de-emphasize his career to have more time with his family might well be making the correct choice. That said, the choice should be made consciously and with the recognition that attempting to hold a business career in place often results in it sliding backwards. Just ask a few of the many women who have juggled a career with starting a family. Most would agree that they are making the right choice but it usually comes at a price.

From *Good Enough* to Tough Times and Back Again

As you see, *Good Enough* can be a serious problem—especially when it runs smack into the wall of tough times. At first blush, you would think that massive reversals would cause *Good Enough* to quickly disappear as an issue. But often, it doesn't. Rather, it remains as a barrier and a blinder.

In a short, slight downturn it is easy to keep going. There is cash in the bank, food on the table and a reservoir of confidence from past successes. But if the downturn is dramatic or lasts a while, it's easy to fall into a funk. We torment ourselves: "If only I would have. Clearly, I should have and there is no doubt I could have." Woulda, shoulda, coulda!

In such a circumstance, the underlying pessimism that *Good Enough* engenders makes the situation worse. It stops Advisors and their clients from seeing new and different opportunities. Instead, when *Good Enough* meets tough times, there is a tendency to try to return to the good old days, to recreate what was. A perspective riveted on the rear-view mirror rarely works. Looking to the future with fresh eyes is the only answer.

Act: Take Intelligent Risks

As we have discussed, when downturns occur, investors become overly conservative. That causes them to miss the chance to recover and prosper again. Many investors are full of fear and they demand a level of certainty that is simply not available. They wait for the perfect time to reenter, but by the time they realize it has come, it has passed.

As a result, in challenging times the most valuable services an Advisor can provide are to:

Gloves Off Quote
Don't Delay

"Delay always breeds danger. To protract a great design is often to ruin it." – Cervantes

1. Instill in clients the courage and confidence to face the reality of what has happened.
2. Help clients identify what there is to be learned from past missteps.
3. Encourage clients to set new goals and objectives.
4. Embolden clients to take action and move face first into the future. After all, an essential step in achieving any plan is to set it in motion.

All of that takes an Advisor who has dealt with his or her own issues and is ready to take a stand.

It's Not Personal

When events catch you by surprise it can feel very personal, but it usually isn't. Your problems are probably just "collateral damage" from wider events. It is foolhardy and debilitating to think the universe is conspiring against you. Do that and you likely will worry so much that you stop functioning—stop doing your job. Instead, it is best to make the needed adjustments and keep moving forward.

Don't Give Up on Your Goals

Events may not be personal, but your goals certainly are. Don't automatically forfeit them because of a setback. This does not mean putting on rose-colored glasses and ignoring reality. When dealing with a difficult circumstance, you need the ability to assess your situation, the courage to set your course and the discipline to stay that course.

Review your goals and dreams. Modify them. Discard those that have lost their meaning and reprioritize the rest. Do all that, but don't give up your most important goals. If you must, extend the timeline for their completion. If your goal was to accomplish something this year and it is now clear that you won't even get close, set your plans to reach that goal next year, or in two or three years. Keep your goals alive and they will serve your spirit and your business well.

Once you have mapped your course, you must devote yourself to it. Empower your goals with sufficient emotion to compel action. Then assess the situation and set your sights.

It is best to remember to include contingency plans. Ask yourself some basic questions: "What will I do if my assumptions are wrong? How will I attain my goals if the market does not come back any time soon?" When things start to go wrong you won't have time to plan. So, do your planning now. You will have to take quick and decisive action if your original plan can't be seen to fruition. Do what you tell your clients to do: plan ahead.

Finding and Honoring Your Core Values

The process of reviewing your goals, dispensing with those that have lost their meaning and retaining those that are still important will be made much easier if you first look deeper and identify your core values, interests and competencies. In other words, determine the place from which your most meaningful and important goals flow.

Identifying one's core is easy for some, but quite problematical for others. If you fall into the first group, congratulations! If you are in the latter, it is crucial to do the introspective work and plan ahead. During a crisis, quick and decisive action is often required. Laying out detailed plans in advance would be best but few of us have the time to do it. Moreover, when the crisis is caused by unanticipated events and results in unexpected effects sufficient plans will not exist. In that case, it is critical to have carefully defined your core. If you have not, chances are that you will fall into one of two traps. You may become rigid, afraid to take action or change your behavior for fear of cutting into your vaguely defined core. Conversely, you may act in desperation and make changes that cut into your core. In either case, a brooding bitterness and a biting cynicism can result.

To guard against this, take yourself through a process similar to the one you ask your clients to complete. Determine what you value most in your life and your business, what your most meaningful objectives are and where your strengths and weaknesses lie. Then invest a few hours during a calm time to ask yourself "What would I do if …?" questions. If you have trouble doing it yourself, hire a personal coach or counselor to take you through the process.

Be Lofty About Your Contribution

Once you have identified your core and confirmed your direction and goals, you may need to redefine what you do for a living. In other words, reframe the way you think about and describe the contribution you make.

In a complex economy, what each of us does for a living makes a contribution to the whole. Yet, if you ask most people what they do, their chests rarely puff out in pride. Rather, they are likely to put down their chosen calling by inserting an actual or subliminal "just" in front of it: "I am (just) an accountant, (just) a salesperson, (just) an insurance broker, or (just) a Financial Advisor.

When an acquaintance of ours, a successful property and casualty insurance broker, started questioning the meaning and purpose of his life and career we wanted to prove to him the importance of his work. We were surprised by what we found in researching his industry.

Property and casualty insurance traces its history to the confluence of two events:

1. The creation of probability theory in the 16th century by the mathematician and philosopher Blaise Pascal.
2. The rise of the sailing ships and the beginning of world trade.

The ability to calculate probabilities led to the measurement of risk that, in turn, led to the ability to trade risk and spread it.

Before Pascal's theory was put to use, investing in trade was a high risk/high return proposition. If the ship came back loaded with goods, it was a bonanza. If, however, it came back empty or failed to come back, all was lost. Under such conditions, it was difficult for ships' captains to raise all the money they needed to embark on voyages.

A few years after Pascal developed his theory, news of it arrived at Edwin Lloyd's coffee shop on the Thames in London. There, the captains of sailing ships looking for funding for their trading adventures met with wealthy Londoners. With Pascal's theory in hand, they were able to spread the risk by forming groups that would insure cargos against loss. With the birth of Lloyd's of London, a boom in world trade ensued.

Today, property and casualty insurance is every bit as critical to the world economy. Without it, fewer people would own homes and those that did would likely have smaller ones with less elaborate furnishings. With no insurance available, many people would not drive cars, fewer buildings would be built and shipping goods would be more costly. In short, much of the world's economy would grind to a near halt. And our friend thought he was "just" an insurance broker? He is saving the world!—or, at least, making a significant contribution.

We all make a contribution and Advisors make a particularly important one. Recognize your contribution, acknowledge yourself and move on with pride, passion and vigor.

Avoid Being a Disappointed Idealist

The culture in our industry encourages cynicism. We tend to talk tough and laugh at gallows humor. While such behavior can provide a short-term emotional release, when it's allowed to run rampant it can destroy our spirit.

When encountering cynicism in others, try not to focus on all the sneering, fault-finding and sarcasm. While clearly there is insincerity, malevolence and incompetence in the world, it does us little good to gripe about it. Instead, step back and try to perceive the cynic as a disappointed idealist. See him or her as an optimist or even a romantic who has been deeply disappointed by circumstances and events. Treating cynics as idealists is the first step toward helping them recover their true character.

If cynicism is getting you down personally, you can break out of it by rediscovering your ideals and passions. Take some

Gloves Off Story
Saving Lives

At a party a young surgeon pompously announced that his services were worth a fortune because he saves lives. Surgeons do deserve a lot of credit and compensation. They are smart, talented, work hard and go through many years of intense training. But saving lives? Food, shelter and clothing are more essential, so farmers, grocery clerks, clothing manufacturers and homebuilders save more lives.

During the 20th Century life expectancy in the U.S. went from 47 years to nearly 80. Clearly, health-care advances made a significant contribution but most of the increase in life expectancy is attributed to improvements in sanitation and water supply. Arguably then, plumbers, garbage collectors and even automobile manufacturers did more to extend life.

A vivid example: In 1900, New York City had 150,000 horses. Horses produce 20 to 25 pounds of waste a day. A little quick math indicates that 3- to 4-million pounds of animal excrement were deposited on New York's streets every day. And New York was not alone. Back then, big cities were putrid places with garbage in the streets and pigs to eat it. In many cities, the water was so bad that alcohol consumption was considered the healthy alternative. Plumbers have certainly improved our lifestyle and saved lives. (Maybe that's why they charge more than surgeons. ☺)

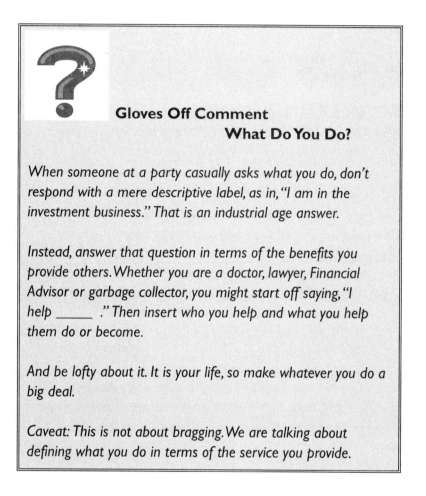

Gloves Off Comment
What Do You Do?

When someone at a party casually asks what you do, don't respond with a mere descriptive label, as in, "I am in the investment business." That is an industrial age answer.

Instead, answer that question in terms of the benefits you provide others. Whether you are a doctor, lawyer, Financial Advisor or garbage collector, you might start off saying, "I help _____ ." Then insert who you help and what you help them do or become.

And be lofty about it. It is your life, so make whatever you do a big deal.

Caveat: This is not about bragging. We are talking about defining what you do in terms of the service you provide.

time. Remember how it was when you were excited about your work? Reignite your imagination and find your confidence. Let the disappointments go and your ideals and passions will rise to the surface again. This time around, you won't be a pie-in-the-sky optimist. Rather, you will be an enthusiastic, passionate and committed Advisor. Below are some ideas to make sure you stay above the fray.

Look for the Ponies

It is easy to be a pessimist. Why not take the "Road Less Traveled"?

Especially when things are difficult, keep a smile on your face and look for the ponies.

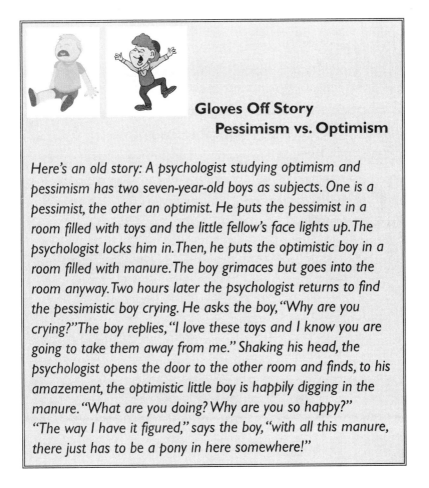

Gloves Off Story
Pessimism vs. Optimism

Here's an old story: A psychologist studying optimism and pessimism has two seven-year-old boys as subjects. One is a pessimist, the other an optimist. He puts the pessimist in a room filled with toys and the little fellow's face lights up. The psychologist locks him in. Then, he puts the optimistic boy in a room filled with manure. The boy grimaces but goes into the room anyway. Two hours later the psychologist returns to find the pessimistic boy crying. He asks the boy, "Why are you crying?" The boy replies, "I love these toys and I know you are going to take them away from me." Shaking his head, the psychologist opens the door to the other room and finds, to his amazement, the optimistic little boy is happily digging in the manure. "What are you doing? Why are you so happy?" "The way I have it figured," says the boy, "with all this manure, there just has to be a pony in here somewhere!"

Keep Some Enjoyment In Your Life

Laughing and playing can be a challenge when times are tough. Yet, humor and joy are not just the "best medicine," they are essential. Take in a movie, go out on the town, go dancing, tell jokes, and laugh!

Get in Shape

There is little doubt that troublesome times can put a lot of stress on the human body. Despite all the demands on your time, and tempting as it may be to take any available moment to kick back and chow down, do all you can to be true to your body. Without it, you can't serve anyone.

Watch what you eat, join a gym, ride a bicycle, play an active sport, go dancing, walk. If you can't trust yourself to exercise regularly, hire an expensive personal trainer. Maybe paying their bill will shame you into doing something. If nothing else works, throw out the TV remote control and get up to change channels!

Gloves Off Story
Shape Up for Stress

What a success story he had been. Long before the days of the dot-commers, he had started his business in college, buying duplexes and fixing them up. By the time he graduated, he was a millionaire. At 30, he was running a huge company and by 35 he was part owner of a big league team. Then the bottom fell out and almost everyone in the business was in deep trouble. Somehow, he survived and he came to the meeting to tell lesser mortals in the business how he had done it. He listed seven keys to his success in averting complete collapse. In keeping with his reputation, his first six keys were logical, orderly and very precise. Good stuff. Then he said: "There is one more thing. It was the most important and rewarding thing I did." He paused and the audience waited anxiously. Then he continued, "I realized that these were going to be very stressful times so I lost 40 pounds and got in shape!"

All of his ideas sounded important at the meeting, but only the last one passed the test of time.

Chapter Seven

Becomimg Emotionally Eloquent

Some say attitude is everything. It isn't. When you are dealing with a challenging state of affairs, you need more than a smile on your face and a song in your heart. You need the acumen to assess your situation, the insight and judgment to set the correct course and the determination and personal discipline to stay that course.

Nevertheless attitudes, emotions and feelings are vital to both Advisors and clients. They create the critical context within which your clients' actions will be determined. In boom times, managing emotions is often demeaned as the "soft side" of the business. In more demanding times, it is perceived as somewhat more important and gets additional attention. In both good times and bad, however, managing emotions is probably the most critical part of an Advisor's function.

It almost goes without saying that an investment strategy, based on a rational long-term view will dramatically outperform a continuously changing strategy based on your own emotional responses to current conditions. Yet, we humans are emotional beings. Feelings, affections, prejudices and passions all have a significant impact on clients and Advisors alike.

Since subjective responses play such a key role in determining investment success or failure, it stands to reason that Advisors must do more than merely understand the technicalities of their field. They must also become emotionally eloquent.

Emotional Eloquence Defined

For Financial Advisors, emotional eloquence means the ability and willingness to:

1. Interpret and understand a client's subjective responses to market conditions and their own,
2. Communicate effectively with the client about the client's responses, and
3. Lead the client back to a rational plan that meets the client's long-term needs and goals.

Attaining emotional eloquence will benefit Advisors by helping them to sense market emotions more keenly. That, in turn, may help them better understand market opportunities and risks.

Conscious Emotional Investing

Here is a rare client: One who makes a conscious choice to rely on hunches, feelings, astrology, numerology, channeling

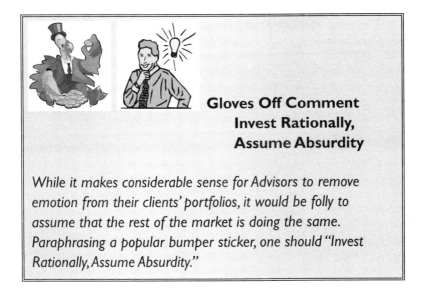

**Gloves Off Comment
Invest Rationally,
Assume Absurdity**

While it makes considerable sense for Advisors to remove emotion from their clients' portfolios, it would be folly to assume that the rest of the market is doing the same. Paraphrasing a popular bumper sticker, one should "Invest Rationally, Assume Absurdity."

and Tarot cards when setting and executing financial strategies. Although the Advisor's role in such a case is clearly tenuous, at least the client's methodology is out in the open for the Advisor to see. In such a circumstance, the Advisor might encourage the client to segregate out a portion of his funds, take them to a discount house and trade on whims and astrological signs. Then, the Advisor might be able to get the rest of the money organized on a rational basis.

Unconscious Emotional Investing

Then there is the great mass of emotional investors who think they are investing rationally. Many of these investors are intelligent and well educated. Their thinking is logical and their methodology may well be precise. Without knowing it, however, they are operating from an emotional context that skews their perceptions and, consequently, their decisions. In this all too common situation, the investors' intelligence, education, logic and reason actually work against them and their portfolios.

Rational Vs. Emotional

It is in exactly these kinds of situations that an emotionally eloquent Advisor can make the most meaningful contributions. To do so, the Advisor must guide the investor in shifting his or her context from their own emotions to reason. After all, a rational context is an investor's best friend. It results in a logical, orderly and accurate processing of information and produces the most reliable answers.

Rationality set in the context of emotions, however, can produce precisely the wrong answer. When one's own greed, fear and other passions place an emotional filter on the free flow of information received by the mind, reason and rational processing can become an investor's worst enemy. This happens when investors believe they are being rational and therefore assume they have reached the correct decision. As a result they are more likely to act on their conclusions.

Emotionally colored information leads to erroneous conclusions. When the conclusions are presumed to have been rationally reached, they gain a credibility that makes them all the more likely to lead to wrong actions.

Gloves Off Comment
Another Use for Emotional Eloquence

If one can rationally assess the emotional reactions of others in advance, successful market timing becomes possible. So all you need to do is become emotionally eloquent, get off the up and down roller coaster and beat the system! Right? Wrong! Reaching that level of emotional eloquence is rare.

During the 1980s and 90s market timing fell out of favor for two major reasons. First, it simply wasn't necessary. Investors only needed to get in and hang on. Equally important, most market timers lost money and many lost big. When the market fell, however, there was renewed interest in market timing.

The developing field of behavioral finance is starting to prove that market timing based on assessments of the emotional reactions of investors can work. Behavioral finance is an offshoot of behavioral economics, a field that is gaining ever more notice. In fact, the Nobel prize in Economics in 2002 was shared by two men who work to explain idiosyncrasies in the way people make supposedly rational economic decisions. Interestingly, one of them was a psychologist, the first to be so lauded.

> Adherents of behavioral finance maintain that while it is irrational to invest based on one's own emotions, it is completely rational, even essential to include the emotions of others in deciding what you should do and when you should do it. Woody Dorsey a behavioral finance expert, summed up his philosophy this way: "Observe everything, believe nothing, and invest only on the basis of the behavioral errors of others."

Garbage In, Garbage Out

When the first computers appeared in investment sales in the 1970's, salespeople proudly showed their clients analysis printed on humongous sheets of computer paper. Because the numbers came out of a computer, people assumed they were accurate and acted on them. Often, however, the numbers were no better than their flawed assumptions. The resulting misjudgments led to a new saying, "*Garbage in, garbage out*".

Stretching the analogy, if one deposits information in a sanitary landfill, it becomes garbage. Most so-called rational models fail to perform because emotions create an erroneous context. When reading the newspaper or watching financial news shows, the majority of people are not gathering information. They are stirring their own emotions and they usually do not know it. After all, most news sources habitually sacrifice accuracy for excitement. They also tend to beat their drum behind the marching band, either feeding the greedy frenzy or fostering the developing climate of fear. As we have discussed, exciting an audience's emotions enhances ratings.

These days, many affluent people start their mornings flipping on the financial news channel to check out the futures. Worse, many allow this news to set the tone for their daily outlook until they get around to checking their stocks on the Internet or asking a lunch partner the great American question: "How's the market doing today?" No wonder there is so much volatility in the markets.

Once the mass of emotion starts moving in the direction of either greed or fear most people only hear and see those things that fit their emotional direction. As a result, they often make precisely the wrong decision and almost always miss opportunities that lie just below the obvious surface.

Being Your Client's Advocate

Being your client's advocate requires wringing their emotion out of the investment decision making process. This starts with the Advisor getting control of his or her own emotions. The Advisor must break out of the same emotional tendencies that lead a client to the wrong decisions.

This is one of the reasons institutional consultants craft carefully worded investment policy statements with trustees of large endowments, foundations and pension plans. Simply put, it not only makes committee members adhere to the plan, but also assures that the consultant remains committed. After all, the consultant is human and is vulnerable to the noises and passions of the moment. Without a required roadmap to follow the consultant might not maintain the requisite fortitude to proceed with emotionally difficult decisions.

In the weeks following September 11, 2001, scores of institutions around the U.S. were rebalancing their investments. They did so not because they were uncaring or greedy, but because their predetermined written investment plans forced their personal upsets and fears aside and allowed rational behavior to prevail.

For this reason, written investment policies should be established for each and every client you advise. The Advisor's job is to unwire his or her client's emotions and break the emotional lock on rational behavior.

Advisors must be able to communicate attentively, forcefully and persuasively to get past their client's reasonable, intellectual mind and deal directly with the client's emotions.

The steps are easy enough. An emotionally eloquent Advisor will do something akin to the following:

1. Listen actively to your client. Don't just wait for him or her to stop talking so you can make your presentation.
2. Patiently ask the client to say more about how he or she feels.
3. To confirm understanding, repeat in your own words what the client has said.

4. Validate the client's emotional logic.
5. Then, with the path opened, offer your more rational approach.

All of this is simple in concept but can require a lot of planning and effort to accomplish. To begin with, it can be time consuming. In addition, it will require skills many Advisors have not had to develop in the past. To their credit, most sales courses stress both listening and persuasion. Clearly, listening is an essential characteristic of emotional eloquence. And, persuasion is an art and science that includes both rational argument and emotional appeal.

In practice, however, pressure to perform—and perform quickly—often reduces listening to a manipulative tool devoid of emotional connection. Persuasion often loses its caring content and becomes a blunt effort to convince clients and prospects to buy.

Emotional eloquence is about getting clients to talk about their hopes, fears, observations and conclusions. It is about them having the confidence in you to reveal the silliest things.

- "But Grandpa told me never to sell IBM."
- "I grew up in a home where it was not all right to make mistakes. If I sell that stock now it will be admitting I was wrong."
- "You're the one who told me to buy this fund. You fix it."

So emotional eloquence is listening with care and caring. It is questioning and confirming with patience and without a manipulative agenda. It is understanding intellectually, validating emotionally, and then decisively moving on to a new and rational plan of action.

Your Client Is Not Your Client

Another compelling reason for you to develop or enhance your emotional eloquence is that the vast majority of your clients are not really your clients. Take your client, Nancy Jones, for example. She is a 50-year-old divorced woman, her daughter is grown, and she has a $1.5 million nest egg from her share of the marital property she and her ex-husband accumulated during their marriage. She has a secure job, earns in the low six figures and enjoys a fine lifestyle. She doesn't need you now. Life is good. In fact, everything you have to offer will require that she forgo current gratification and put money aside. Why should she do that? It is counterintuitive and borders on the insane.

But Nancy, at 50, with money in the bank and a good source of current income is not your client. Your client is Nancy 20 or 30 years from now. Then she will have to rely on her investments to supplement any pension she might have so that she can continue to live the lifestyle to which she has grown accustomed. Your client might also be Nancy's daughter or a grandchild who might need some help during their lives. Understand that more often than not, Nancy at

50 is the enemy of Nancy at 75. Your job is to take care of the elder Nancy even if it means confronting the younger when necessary. Frequently, you will be the elder client's only advocate. So, understanding them and their emotions is essential to serving them. In other words, it is simply your job.

Empowering Yourself

Chapter Eight

Understanding Client Emotions

While academic types have written volumes on the subject, those of us who have been in the field know that much of the story can be told in just two words—greed and fear.

The Violent Swing from Greed to Fear and Back Again

It may be a law of nature: when investors should be most fearful, greed rules, and when they should be grabbing up bargains, they run for the exits.

As the market soars, greed dominates investors' emotions, clouds their judgment and overshadows their vision. It is not just that these investors have difficulty seeing possible risks. It is a much more serious situation. For such investors, near certainty of loss masquerades as an exciting opportunity for great gain: the proverbial *sure thing*. Many even seem to equate enormous risk with intelligence, courage and high returns. When the market is at its peak, one of the best-known and effective sales techniques is "over-full" disclosure. The more a promoter emphasizes that an investment is really risky, the more the greed-stricken investor wants to commit.

Once major losses have been realized, however, the opposite is true. Having learned that risk can indeed mean RISK, most investors either freeze and do nothing, or dive for their cash. At both the top and the bottom, only a handful have the presence of mind and the courage to rebalance their portfolios in accordance with their long-term goals. As a result, most leave themselves over-exposed at the top and under-invested at the bottom. Consequently, few fully capitalize on their investments over the long haul. After a bust, by the time most investors regain their mettle and get back in the game, they are too late and so the fear-greed-fear cycle continues.

Why do so few of us learn from our mistakes? Why do so few buy at or near the bottom and so many of us sell at or near the top? Learning from our mistakes—or better, from the mistakes of others—is perhaps the best way to become adept at managing our reactions to the ebbs and flows within the markets and among the various asset classes.

Even after it becomes clear that what we did in the past made no sense why do so many of us do it again and again? One answer is that our past actions actually did make sense . . . emotional sense.

Another answer to this behavioral conundrum is that so few of us read history. We think that our time is the first time, that what is happening to us now has never happened to anyone before. In that fallacy lies our problem. Even those who are aware of history can fall into the same trap. After all, the realities of history are a feeble match for the emotional momentum of a rapidly rising or frantically falling market.

Gloves Off Comment
Fall Off the Floor?

When a given market or asset class is hitting new highs, nearly everyone wants a piece of the action that has already passed them by. Ask why and most clients will tell you it is a great investment. When that same market or asset class is deeply depressed and available for fire-sale prices, few want to buy. Ask why and they will say the investment is too risky.

Risky? How does one fall off the floor?

Perhaps we would all be better off retailing consumer products. When retailers have a sale, more people buy. In the often irrational world of investing that just doesn't happen. That is where the opportunity lies.

In a bull market, our ignorance and arrogance combine to dominate our collective psyche. Anyone mentioning the lessons learned in other boom/bust cycles will be on the receiving end of a look usually reserved for benevolent idiots. And on the receiving end of remarks such as, "How can you say that? This is a new age, a new economy. Things are fundamentally different."

Clearly, no two ages are the same. Some things really do

change radically and fundamentally. Technology is a clear example. Throughout history, technological inventions have changed the way people live and work. And those advances have been coming ever more rapidly. Yet, values, habits, cultures and behavior change only gradually. Perhaps that is why Mark Twain's comment about history rhyming seems so appropriate a century later. History does rhyme and it does so repeatedly. Your client's investment strategies must take that rhyming into account.

The Value in Feeling the Pain

In moving toward mastering an activity, the question isn't will you make mistakes. The question is what will you do with the mistakes you make.

After making a major error, there is usually an understandable desire to end the pain quickly. As a result, there is a strong tendency to move on as quickly as possible. To do this, both individuals and organizations are prone to hastily making rules that will prevent them from making the same mistakes in the future.

After a crisis, businesses turn to their legal and accounting departments to develop more restrictive policies and more detailed rulebooks. Governments, under pressure to do something quickly, promulgate Draconian rules designed to eliminate past abuses.

While individuals usually are less formal in their process,

they are no less prolific in their rule making. "I'll never do it that way again." "I will always do it this way."

In certain circumstances such rule making makes sense. There are situations and conditions that should be ruled out quickly. That said, rule making has problems. To begin with, such rules rarely foreclose future problems. For example, the laws and regulations created to prevent fraud and abuse after the savings and loan crisis in the 1980's did little to limit the financial reporting and auditing abuses that surfaced in 2002.

In addition, rules that are designed to solve problems often become problems themselves. The best examples probably lie in health care, where so many treatments have what are euphemistically referred to as side effects. On the regulatory side, catalytic converters were required in cars to reduce smog. Now there is evidence they increase global warming. On a personal level, people installed car alarms to stop thieves from stealing their cars while parked. Since the thieves could not get the cars while parked, there was soon a rash of car-jackings. Thieves took our cars while we were in them.

Perhaps an even more serious consequence of such rule making is that, over time, rules squelch flexibility, stifle creativity and limit productivity.

Equally as important, ending a situation by rushing to make rules obscures or eliminates any lessons that might be learned. As Nietzsche put it, we "disturb the good digestion of the experience. Instead of wisdom, ... (we) acquire indigestion."

In his model for developing competence, the philosopher Hubert Dreyfus offers an alternative to rule making: feel the pain. In other words, mull the mistake or miscalculation over and over, relive it again and again, piece it apart, until it is fully digested and all of its lessons are revealed. Unlike simple, straightforward rule making, "feeling of the pain" is not necessarily linear. It operates at many levels: the linear level of the rational mind, the many machinations of the emotional mind and the often-circuitous workings of the heart and soul. The process takes time and it hurts, but that is where the real lessons lie.

A Dangerous Combination

As we have discussed, most investors operate out of an emotional context and are devoid of historical perspective. In addition, as a culture we place an extraordinary degree of importance on money, not only as a way of buying goods and services but also as valuing our worth as human beings. This makes for an explosive combination that can lead to very expensive consequences, both financially and emotionally.

In much of the old world, acceptance of an individual is still a birthright. People know who they are and what their place is in the community. In the developed world, and especially in the United States, our freedom and mobility leave many of us living far from our birthplace and our identity. Many of us follow our hearts as we head for places and people unknown. Once we're there, we need to establish ourselves in our new community. One of the primary ways we do that is by doing things that require money.

Money matters a lot in our society. For better or worse money goes a long way to defining who we are and where we stand in our community. Virtually no one likes losing money. When clients lose 20% of their capital, Advisors must understand that their clients' self-image may be in jeopardy. In other words, it is not just the money. It is their concept of who they are. It may even be their standing in the community that is at risk.

Conversely, when times are good clients can easily get full of themselves and start thinking they have the Midas touch. Then, often at the time when markets are most risky, they place bigger and bigger bets. Perhaps that is why so few investors are willing to take their chips off the table when they are on a winning streak.

The analogy to casinos is an easy way to communicate to clients that a rational investor can do very well over time. It requires being in the game, playing for a long time and having at least a small advantage over the other players.

Sinking in Sunk Costs

The flip side of not being able to get up and leave the table when one is winning is not being able to let go of a loser. High on the list of silly things investors say is, "I can't sell that investment now. If I do, I will have a loss!" Clearly, they already have the loss. They just don't want to face it.

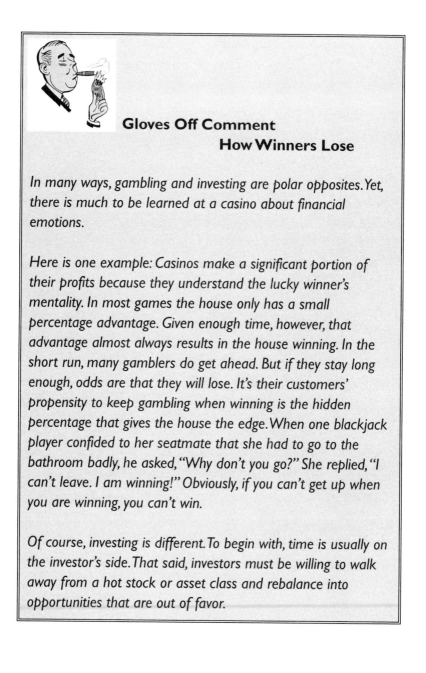

Gloves Off Comment
How Winners Lose

In many ways, gambling and investing are polar opposites. Yet, there is much to be learned at a casino about financial emotions.

Here is one example: Casinos make a significant portion of their profits because they understand the lucky winner's mentality. In most games the house only has a small percentage advantage. Given enough time, however, that advantage almost always results in the house winning. In the short run, many gamblers do get ahead. But if they stay long enough, odds are that they will lose. It's their customers' propensity to keep gambling when winning is the hidden percentage that gives the house the edge. When one blackjack player confided to her seatmate that she had to go to the bathroom badly, he asked, "Why don't you go?" She replied, "I can't leave. I am winning!" Obviously, if you can't get up when you are winning, you can't win.

Of course, investing is different. To begin with, time is usually on the investor's side. That said, investors must be willing to walk away from a hot stock or asset class and rebalance into opportunities that are out of favor.

Some Advisors may exacerbate the situation. Going along with the idea that a paper loss is somehow not a loss can placate a client in the short term. In the longer run, it reinforces the tendency toward irrationality.

The preferred course is for Advisors and their clients to *feel the pain* of past mistakes and move on. Only in that way can portfolios be reallocated in accordance with a rational long-term plan.

Become Client Intimate

"Client Intimacy" is not something that just happens. All clients formulate views from a combination of their heart, mind and stomach. Your role is to step into each of these areas and help clients formulate a game plan that is in sync with all three. Different clients process information and emotions differently. Your success will be determined by how well you understand, acknowledge and take into account each individual's way of processing.

We all come to the table with a tremendous amount of baggage regarding our views of money. "My parents had nothing," "My parents had everything," "My parents had everything and lost it all," and all combinations thereof. In marriages, the baggage is usually not a matching set.

In many cases, it is the Advisor's job to be a financial therapist, to listen to what is not said and to watch for and point out inconsistencies and other potential problems.

The Soft Side Isn't Soft

In much of our society, the human side is downplayed, even disparaged. For many, technology and science rule. Yet a substantial portion of an Advisor's role is simply being there for clients: providing human contact, confidence and concern is important any time. In a difficult situation this so-called soft side is critical.

As we have discussed, in financial services, the way an Advisor manages a client's emotions is often the difference between success and failure. That is also true in medicine, where managing a patient's emotions can mean the difference between life and death. Yet, over the years the pressures of both science and finance have made it more and more difficult for these care-givers and Advisors to do that part of their job.

Active Listening

Active listening is not only essential, it should be what a client contact is primarily about. It's certainly not about your next appointment, or rushing off to your daughter's basketball game. It is about right here, right now. It's about them, not you; their needs, not your services. It's about being in the moment, but it is more. It's focusing entirely on your clients or prospects. Make the one you are with the only person on the planet for the time you are with him or her. It works for salespeople, politicians and, yes, even lovers. Who can resist someone who sees you as the only person in the world?

Gloves Off Story
The Doctor Who Cared and Was There

When I was a kid, old Doctor Metz was there for us ... at his office when we could, but at our house when we needed him. When I was sick, he would come to the house with his little black bag, sit next to the bed and comfort me. He would hear my tale of woe as he warmed his stethoscope with his hands. Then he would listen to my chest and look up past his bushy eyebrows in a ponderous moment. Finally he would put his hand on my arm, smile warmly and let me know I would be all right.

When my brother hurt his leg Dr. Metz arrived with the ambulance. When at age 50, Dad got pneumonia and almost died, Dr. Metz sat with him all night in the hospital room. Imagine how my mother felt when she got back to the hospital at seven in the morning and found an unshaven, red-eyed Dr. Metz sitting there with Dad, holding his hand, watching him and letting him know there was hope.

In fairness, today's doctors are overwhelmed with pressures that never concerned Dr. Metz. Back then, it was easier to keep up with the slower pace of technological advance, HMOs didn't exist and the trial lawyers weren't suing everyone in sight. Granted, today's doctors do practice better science than old Dr. Metz. Daily they perform miracles about which he could only dream. But, if I got sick and he was still around, I would want him at my bedside. Wouldn't you? Think of Dr. Metz when advising your clients.

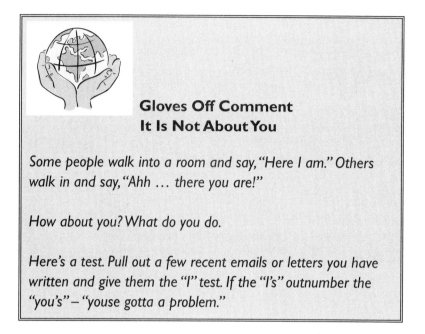

Gloves Off Comment
It Is Not About You

Some people walk into a room and say, "Here I am." Others walk in and say, "Ahh ... there you are!"

How about you? What do you do.

Here's a test. Pull out a few recent emails or letters you have written and give them the "I" test. If the "I's" outnumber the "you's" – "youse gotta a problem."

Understanding and treating a client in this way will help you diagnose the effects of a client's emotions and thoughts. For example, it will help you determine if his or her new-found conservatism is a result of a fundamental shift in attitude or a short-lived reaction to a bull or bear market. That assessment should have a significant impact on your recommendations. The likelihood the client will accept your recommendations and stick with them will be apparent in the results that you produce for him or her over time.

That difference is critical. If you help the client to confront his or her true feelings and adjust your presentation in accordance with the client's needs, you will have a client for life. Moreover, that client is not only more likely to become a significant source of referrals, he or she might just become a passionate advocate. On the other hand, failing to diagnose a client's thoughts and emotions will have a detrimental effect on performance, retention and referrals.

A Written Policy May Not be Enough

A written investment policy is an important tool in keeping clients disciplined. It is created in a rational, orderly manner and can help you maintain that order and rationality in an emotional time. Yet, even with a written investment policy in hand, investors and Advisors are not home free. The ability to confront and control the violent swings between fear and greed remains a critical dimension of the Advisor's role. Fulfilling this role requires a personalized approach, vigilance and resolve. While the fear-greed-fear cycle seems to be an almost universal phenomenon for clients, each person's struggle to override these and other emotions will be different. Taking a personalized approach will require time to perfect.

For example, each individual has a personal threshold of risk when it comes to losing money. One of an Advisor's most important tasks is to determine where that threshold lies for each client. The threshold should not be seen as a relative issue. For example, "Sara and Shawn have a much higher tolerance for loss of capital than most of my other clients."

Relative conclusions are of very little help in treating an individual client's condition.

The focus should instead be on the couple's unique threshold of risk or pain. The individual ability to handle the violent swings of fear and greed need to be based on personal formulas. For example: The pain that Sara and Shawn experience when they lose $50,000 is equal in intensity to the joy they experience when gaining $200,000.

When Advisors fail to focus on the heart of the issues and the client, a superficial, boilerplate diagnosis of risk tolerance often results. After all, deep-seated client perceptions are often masked by the momentary movement of the market. When the market shifts, the superficially diagnosed client wants to shift with it. This leads to an almost sure-to-fail strategy and, ultimately, to a failed Advisory relationship. In your role as a diagnostician, your assessment of your client's risk tolerance may be the most vital function. Master these skills the way a gifted doctor does and your client will place you on a pedestal too.

One of the basic tenets of rational investing is first to determine one's needs, goals, objectives and risk tolerances. Next develop a plan to allocate assets in accordance with percentages that are most likely to meet one's needs. Then, as some asset classes grow in relative value and others shrink, to periodically move funds to rebalance the portfolio. Institutions do it all the time, but few individual investors do. They should.

Some important lessons to be gleaned from the mistakes

Gloves Off Idea
The Right Lesson

Assume an investor, Susan, with $1 million, decides to allocate 60% in growth stocks and 40% in bonds. At the end of the year, the stock market has doubled and bonds are flat. Now the investor has a $1.6 million portfolio, with $1.2 million in stocks and $400,000 in bonds. But that is 75% in stocks and 25% in bonds.

The investor's portfolio is now out of balance and should be reallocated. Susan should sell $240,000 in stocks and buy bonds. That would leave her back in balance with $960,000 in stocks and $640,000 in bonds. Few do, however, because they have decided that stocks are good and bonds are bad. They are more likely to sell bonds and buy more stocks.

Then, let's assume a devastating correction occurs and her stock account falls to $500,000 while her bonds rise to $550,000. Even though she is still ahead, our investor is likely to be crestfallen and will probably make and live by the wrong rules.

Thinking that the lesson is that stocks are bad or that small investors don't have a chance, they might just get out of stocks altogether.

Most Advisors would discourage them from doing that. They would counsel, "Hang tough and it will come back." But hanging tough is not enough. Clients should be rebalancing. In this case, the client should be selling bonds and buying more stocks.

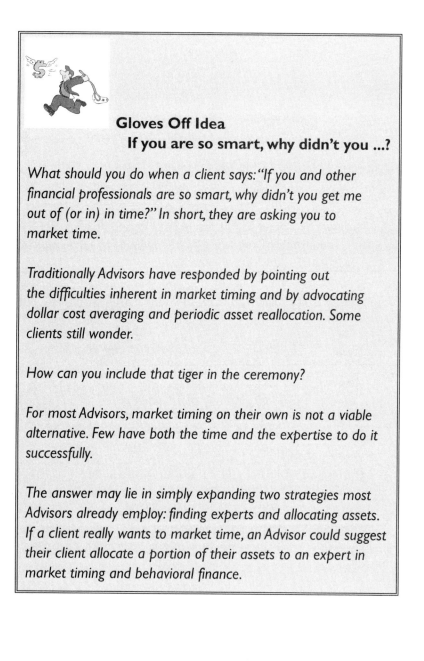

Gloves Off Idea
If you are so smart, why didn't you ...?

What should you do when a client says: "If you and other financial professionals are so smart, why didn't you get me out of (or in) in time?" In short, they are asking you to market time.

Traditionally Advisors have responded by pointing out the difficulties inherent in market timing and by advocating dollar cost averaging and periodic asset reallocation. Some clients still wonder.

How can you include that tiger in the ceremony?

For most Advisors, market timing on their own is not a viable alternative. Few have both the time and the expertise to do it successfully.

The answer may lie in simply expanding two strategies most Advisors already employ: finding experts and allocating assets. If a client really wants to market time, an Advisor could suggest their client allocate a portion of their assets to an expert in market timing and behavioral finance.

we make in a bull market and the opportunities we miss in a bear market are:

1. Markets over steer, often radically.
2. Never underestimate greed at the top or fear at the bottom.
3. Judging the emotional reaction of others can be a very valuable investment management tool.
4. Do not give too much counsel to your own fears. They are about as reliable as a Weegie board.
5. When listening to investment advice from the media, be careful to separate fact from emotion.
6. A written investment policy established in quiet time and in an unemotional way is key.
7. Rebalancing in both good times and bad is important.

If there is a single, important lesson to be learned from the experience of living through a few bull and bear markets, it is this: The biblical admonition, "This too shall pass," applies to both good times and bad.

Chapter Nine

Communicating with Clients

A few basic rules of communications and sales to incorporate into your advisory activities are in order. While these rules apply in both good times and bad, let's look at them from a negative perspective. You have struggled through the depths of a difficult market. You have agonized over the fall and analyzed the mistakes you and your clients made. After you learned the lessons, you healed thyself and even worked toward becoming ever more emotionally eloquent. Now you stand ready to face the world, your clients and new prospects. Everything is in place except that the vast majority of your clients and prospects are refusing to do what you think they should. Now what do you do? Quit? Change careers? Sell shoes? Or rededicate yourself to this calling?

So you decide to stay in the game; what do you do next? Sorry. There are no magic formulas or quick fixes. The answer is to stick with the basics and keep working them. Yes, the basics can be boring but the one thing you can say about them is that they work—in good times and especially in difficult times.

Gloves Off Comment
Become a Shoe Salesperson

Don't rule it out. The shoe business makes sense. If you mark down the price of shoes, people buy more of them. They are rational. When there is an investment sale, however, precious few want to buy.

One key to long-term investment success is to diversify by position in the investment cycle. In other words, buy things when they make good business sense and get rid of them when everyone else thinks they are fantastic investments.

The problem is that few clients are willing to go along. Most investors will not get in a ship that is moored at the dock. They wait until it pulls out to sea, jump in the water and swim after it! Then they wonder why they got soaked.

So, you could sell shoes. But, not so fast—feet can smell worse than WorldCom's books. Perhaps we should rethink that.

ESTABLISH YOUR CREDIBILITY

There is nothing like an *erosion of trust* to remind us of the importance of credibility. When you are credible, people listen. When you are not, they either ignore you or test you. Remember how it was when you first started out? You wanted to know the answer to every question clients were asking. Most likely, your thirst for knowledge was based on more than just your desire to establish relationships and make sales. You probably didn't want to appear a fool. But then an odd thing happened. When you learned the answers to most all the questions, clients and prospects stopped asking them and started requesting your opinions and your guidance. Then, mistakes were made and money was lost and here are those questions again, often with a hard edge. The solution is to rebuild your credibility with your clients and prospects. Don't be discouraged if that takes a while. The problem remains that credibility can be lost in an instant but takes a long time to build.

First and foremost, you must establish credibility with yourself. If you are new in the business, that means learning your craft and perhaps getting designations or other credentials to prove it. If you are suffering a loss of confidence, start by reminding yourself that the lessons you learned from the mistakes you made are actually a credential for moving forward. It is critical that you understand, both intellectually and emotionally, that you are valuable. You are valuable in spite of the mistakes you have made and because of them.

Trite as it may sound, one really does learn best from the tough times. Those lessons are a credential and an important element of the value you offer your future clients.

Once you have reestablished your credibility with yourself, start getting clients and prospects to see the new you.

KNOW YOUR PRODUCT

Clearly, as an Advisor, you must know each investment you offer and every investment strategy you recommend. While knowing your product does not necessarily mean knowing every last detail, it does require that you fully understand the risks and benefits, the tax and planning implications and who should buy and who shouldn't.

Your product, however, is much more than the investments and strategies you offer. It is everything you and your firm do and are. Think of a grocery store. In a narrow sense its product is food, but a consumer's decision about to where to shop is based on a much broader definition of the product. It includes location, access, parking, ease of checkout, variety, cleanliness, personnel and a lot more. In financial services, the product is a bundle of services and competencies. Clearly, the Advisor is a major portion of the product. Your ability, integrity and concern for your client's welfare are the core of your product.

Develop one or more trademark phrases that describe what you do in terms of the benefits to your clients and prospects. Come up with some that are likely to appeal to

Gloves Off Comment
Building Credibility:
Set an Outrageous Goal

Try this one:"I want to become so credible that affluent people will call me and ask for my help in these difficult times. No more selling, they just do what I tell them to do. Then they tell their friends about me."

Now this will take a while, so think long term: Any time you have a decision to make, ask yourself what would be best short term and what would be best long term. You will find that the short-term response is often the exact opposite of the long term.

We don't have to get fancy here. When a waiter or waitress asks if you want that fattening dessert the answer should be, "Short term, yes, but long term, no."

them or at least pique their interest. Be creative. Be lofty. Have fun with it.

So ... accountants are not numbers nerds. They are "interpreters of our quantifiable cultural values." Real estate brokers don't just sell houses. They "create a context in which people can successfully raise their children and live their lives." That corn grower is not just a farmer. He "helps people feed their families, sweeten their sodas and even de-ice their roads. And you are not just a Financial Advisor. You "help, enable, assist, empower, facilitate and support people in living fuller, happier and more secure lives."

KNOW YOUR CLIENT

In a difficult market, knowing one's client begins by calling them or better yet, visiting with them. While it is understandable that as an Advisor you sometimes want to lay low, your job is to be out there with clients and prospects.

But what should you say when you don't know what to say? If you don't know what to say then do what you should be doing most of the time anyway, LISTEN. Listen with your head and your heart. Hear what they need and want.

Not having something to say isn't all bad. In fact, a good rule of thumb in both good times and bad is to speak only when it promotes progress.

Think of every client and prospect as a consultant who is giving you free advice. Listen and make notes. Then get the details into digital form. Make note of it all: their hopes, dreams, and frustrations; their affinity for or fear of numbers and technicalities; whether they like to hear good news first or get the bad news out on the table. Get a sense of how they will react to your recommendations at different times.

Going beyond passive listening to active listening means

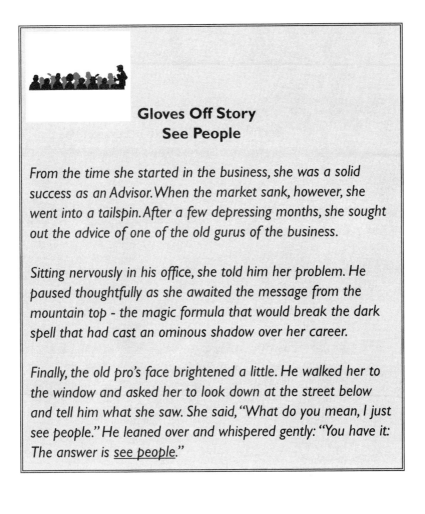

Gloves Off Story
See People

From the time she started in the business, she was a solid success as an Advisor. When the market sank, however, she went into a tailspin. After a few depressing months, she sought out the advice of one of the old gurus of the business.

Sitting nervously in his office, she told him her problem. He paused thoughtfully as she awaited the message from the mountain top - the magic formula that would break the dark spell that had cast an ominous shadow over her career.

Finally, the old pro's face brightened a little. He walked her to the window and asked her to look down at the street below and tell him what she saw. She said, "What do you mean, I just see people." He leaned over and whispered gently: "You have it: The answer is <u>see people</u>."

asking questions that get your clients to talk. It often helps to first restate what they are saying to make sure you understand it and then ask questions that bring them out. Be careful here. If you ask questions just to get information you can later use to manipulate a client, you won't get the whole

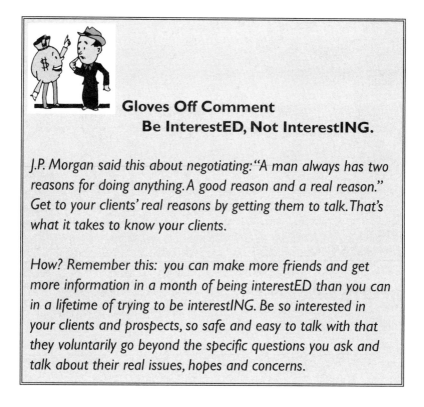

Gloves Off Comment
Be InterestED, Not InterestING.

J.P. Morgan said this about negotiating: "A man always has two reasons for doing anything. A good reason and a real reason." Get to your clients' real reasons by getting them to talk. That's what it takes to know your clients.

How? Remember this: you can make more friends and get more information in a month of being interestED than you can in a lifetime of trying to be interestING. Be so interested in your clients and prospects, so safe and easy to talk with that they voluntarily go beyond the specific questions you ask and talk about their real issues, hopes and concerns.

story for long. The trick is to be genuinely interested in the client. To be effective long term, fact finding must be sincere.

KEEP IT SIMPLE

Advisors who want to inform, motivate, empower and inspire should keep it simple. What's more, the truth is usually simple anyway. The Pythagorean theorem, Archimedes'

Principle, the Lord's Prayer and the Ten Commandments are all succinct, simple and profound.

The ability to communicate complex issues in a simple manner is a critical part of an Advisor's role. When working to make things simple, it is important to avoid making them simplistic or superficial. The key is to understand something so well that you discover its inherent simplicity, its essence, and then communicate that.

If simplicity is so valuable, why do so many of us make things more complex than they need be? Here are a few reasons:

1. **It's Hard Work.** It takes a lot of work to make things simple. It requires a deep understanding of the subject and an intellectual self-assurance.

2. **The Desire to Impress.** The insecure part of us has a strong tendency to want to show whatever knowledge we have. We hope we will prevent others from finding out that we really aren't all that knowledgeable.

3. **Compliance Issues.** No doubt, a heavily regulated industry has a burden to bear. Even though full disclosure has a way of becoming so lengthy and complex that it results in little or no effective disclosure, the rules of the game demand it. However, that makes the Advisor's role as simplifier all the more important.

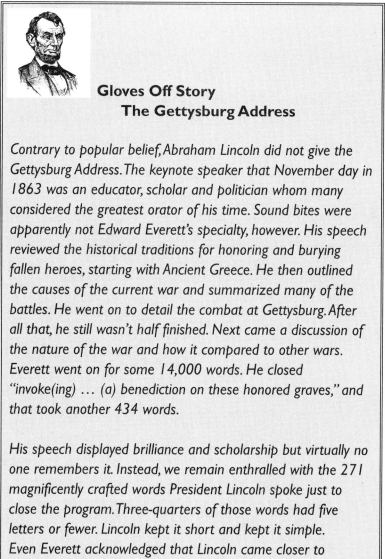

Gloves Off Story
The Gettysburg Address

Contrary to popular belief, Abraham Lincoln did not give the Gettysburg Address. The keynote speaker that November day in 1863 was an educator, scholar and politician whom many considered the greatest orator of his time. Sound bites were apparently not Edward Everett's specialty, however. His speech reviewed the historical traditions for honoring and burying fallen heroes, starting with Ancient Greece. He then outlined the causes of the current war and summarized many of the battles. He went on to detail the combat at Gettysburg. After all that, he still wasn't half finished. Next came a discussion of the nature of the war and how it compared to other wars. Everett went on for some 14,000 words. He closed "invoke(ing) … (a) benediction on these honored graves," and that took another 434 words.

His speech displayed brilliance and scholarship but virtually no one remembers it. Instead, we remain enthralled with the 271 magnificently crafted words President Lincoln spoke just to close the program. Three-quarters of those words had five letters or fewer. Lincoln kept it short and kept it simple. Even Everett acknowledged that Lincoln came closer to capturing the meaning of the moment in two minutes than he had in two hours.

4. **We Are Right, But Can't Prove It.** When you can't find a single compelling reason a client should do something, you have an understandable urge to overload them with lots of reasons or complexities. As the physicist Richard Feynman put it, "I could not think of a good reason, so I gave them five."

5. **We Are Not Certain Why Something Works.** Or we are not certain which argument will appeal to a given client. So we load them up. Uncertainty breeds complexity.

A few Quick Steps to Simplicity

1. **Down to Earth:** Never use big words and fancy phrases when simple words will do.

2. **Think:** If it takes a lot of big words or complex formulas to express a thought, give it more thought.

3. **Shorter is Better:** Vice President Hubert Humphrey's wife, Muriel, put it best when she told her husband, "Your speech does not need to be eternal to be immortal."

4. **Avoid Creeping Growth:** Presentations have a way of growing gradually. You prepare the perfect 15-minute sales presentation and it works. But a week later there is an article in *The Wall Street Journal* that you really like and you add it. It will only take a

couple of minutes, but now you have a 17-minute presentation that you are rushing to complete. And so it grows ...

5. **The Purpose of Analysis:** Most of us think the purpose of analysis is to find answers. It isn't. Rather the purpose is to narrow down the area in which you guess. Clearly that is important. You want to use your intuition in the smallest area possible. Do not kid yourself, however. In the end, you are guessing. When you understand that even the most detailed analysis is based on guesses about the future, you begin to understand the importance of the emotional eloquence discussed earlier.

6. **Get It Down to Six Words:** Here's an exercise that will focus your thoughts. Anytime you have something important about which to communicate, sum up your entire presentation in six words or a six-word phrase. For example, one might explain a variable annuity that has a guaranteed return floor with the words, "upside, safety, comfort, tax benefit, diversification". It's tough, but you can do it.

EMPHASIZE CONCEPTS AND BENEFITS

Industrial salespeople present all the features of their products or services. That makes sense when selling tangible widgets to

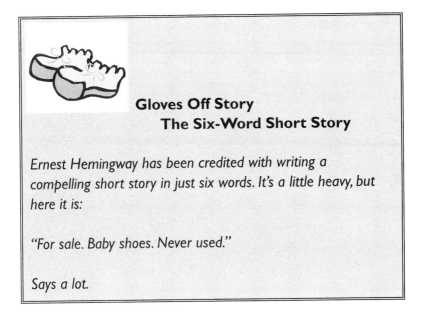

Gloves Off Story
The Six-Word Short Story

Ernest Hemingway has been credited with writing a compelling short story in just six words. It's a little heavy, but here it is:

"For sale. Baby shoes. Never used."

Says a lot.

engineers. If you are advising individuals on financial strategies, however, you should emphasize concepts and benefits.

What is the difference? Features are the specifications: the fine points of "Clause 17c" in an annuity contract; the specifics of the tax assumptions underlying the historical rate of return of a mutual fund; and the precise methodology of the discoveries behind a biotech company's new product. In other words, features aim more at the head—the analytical side of the brain. They are important and an Advisor should understand them before making his or her recommendations to clients. That said, sales and relationships are not built on features. They are built on concepts.

Concepts, or benefits, are less specific. They aim more at the heart and the gut and less at the head. Concepts include such things as value-added service, quality, trust and commitment. Specifics tend to confuse. Concepts tend to motivate.

In moving from features to concepts, take a hint from the advertisers of consumer products. Pick up any consumer-oriented magazine and you will note the use of concepts and benefits. Think of how these products are successfully promoted by Madison Avenue. There is little doubt they have succeeded in getting us to reorder our priorities to favor some products over others.

Its Pepsi inviting customers to "Join the Pepsi Generation, Feelin' Free"; car companies promising to make men more manly; and Virginia Slims seducing young women into thinking that smoking their cigarettes will make them assertive, sexy and strong. The list goes on but the bottom line is that by altering the buying attitudes and values of consumers, Madison Avenue reduced or eliminated the need to have salespeople "sell" products. Once we humans think we need something, we seek it out.

The bottom line for Advisors is this: disclose the facts and figures; stress concepts and benefits and do it with enthusiasm, certainty and commitment.

TAKE A CHANCE

As the world changes and the markets move, it is clearly best to stay ahead of the curve. Few of us seem to be able to con-

**Gloves Off Comment
"Avoiding Advice But Sold On Soap"**

Financial advice still has to be sold while bath soap is bought. In large part that is because soap and many other consumer products have been so well marketed on the basis of concepts and benefits.

When the household runs low on bath soap we get in the car, drive to the store, retrieve the soap off the shelf and stand in line to pay for it. No salesperson need call. After all, we <u>need</u> soap. We shower or bathe almost everyday. But why? Mainly because we have been marketed the idea of a daily bath being essential both physically and socially.

Just a few generations ago, most North Americans got their water from a well in the backyard—one bucket at a time. How often would you bathe if you had to carry one bucket at a time and heat the water over a wood stove? Now, we're told we need to bathe often and we need soap.

More to the point, if Advisors 100 years ago had been marketing concepts and benefits, perhaps people would have settled for a bath every third day and used the time saved to plan their finances!

Use concepts and benefits to show people they need financial advice just as much as they need soap.

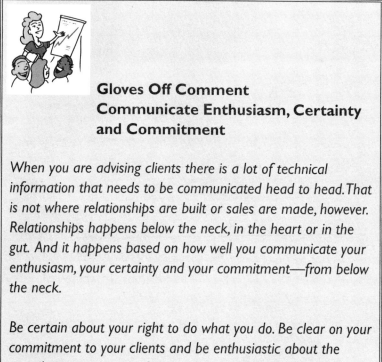

Gloves Off Comment
Communicate Enthusiasm, Certainty and Commitment

When you are advising clients there is a lot of technical information that needs to be communicated head to head. That is not where relationships are built or sales are made, however. Relationships happens below the neck, in the heart or in the gut. And it happens based on how well you communicate your enthusiasm, your certainty and your commitment—from below the neck.

Be certain about your right to do what you do. Be clear on your commitment to your clients and be enthusiastic about the contribution you are making to them.

sistently do that. In fact, it is quite an accomplishment to just keep pace with the changes around us.

Why? In part it is because we have been successful in the past. It is observably true that the smarter people are, the more successful they are. The better educated they are, the harder it is for them to change. After all, they did well the old way and are understandably attached to it. That is one of the reasons that yesterday's geniuses often become tomorrow's fools.

In these volatile times, it is critical to continually re-energize yourself, to change and expand what you do and the way you do it. Doing and being more requires that you do things in non-habitual ways.

Breaking the powerful lure of doing things the familiar way does not come naturally to most of us. To do so, you will need to consciously put yourself into situations that make you think and feel differently. In other words, you will have to manage yourself.

You can start by doing a lot of little things: have your family change seats at the dinner table; wear your watch on other hand; drive a new route to work or, better, use a different form of transportation; take up a musical instrument; try a new sport; join a new club; whatever.

Then try putting yourself at risk in front of clients. Think about it. When are we most creative? Isn't it when we are new in a business or activity. That's when everything is fresh and exciting. It is also when we are at the greatest risk of making fools of ourselves in front of others. The desire to avoid humiliation inspires creativity. After we have been in the business a while we get so good at it that we are seldom concerned—and rarely inspired or creative.

Take chances and put yourself at risk. That is when the ideas flow.

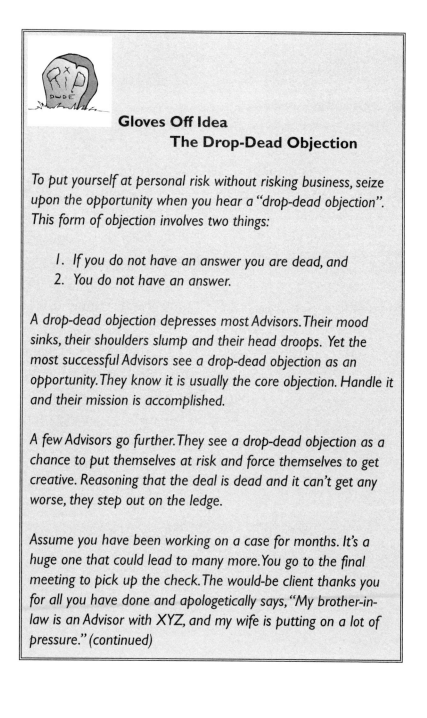

Gloves Off Idea
The Drop-Dead Objection

To put yourself at personal risk without risking business, seize upon the opportunity when you hear a "drop-dead objection". This form of objection involves two things:

1. *If you do not have an answer you are dead, and*
2. *You do not have an answer.*

A drop-dead objection depresses most Advisors. Their mood sinks, their shoulders slump and their head droops. Yet the most successful Advisors see a drop-dead objection as an opportunity. They know it is usually the core objection. Handle it and their mission is accomplished.

A few Advisors go further. They see a drop-dead objection as a chance to put themselves at risk and force themselves to get creative. Reasoning that the deal is dead and it can't get any worse, they step out on the ledge.

Assume you have been working on a case for months. It's a huge one that could lead to many more. You go to the final meeting to pick up the check. The would-be client thanks you for all you have done and apologetically says, "My brother-in-law is an Advisor with XYZ, and my wife is putting on a lot of pressure." (continued)

If you can't think of anything better to say, try, "That's exactly why you ought to be working with me." And wait. The client will probably say "Huh." Unless you think of something better, assume he did not hear you and slowly repeat yourself, saying, "That's exactly why you should be working with me." Wait again.

There is a small chance the objection will just fade away but more likely the client will say, "What do you mean by that?" If nothing creative has burst into your brain, try, "You know!" Maybe the client will say, "You mean my brother-in-law is a fool?" or "You mean it is easy to hire my brother-in-law but impossible to fire him?" Then you only need agree and move on.

But what if the potential client says, "No. I do not know what you mean. What do you mean?" At this point, all we have to offer is "some book suggested I try this."

Whatever you come up with will be better than that! It might even be brilliant. After all, avoidance of humiliation is indeed a terrific motivator. If you get lucky, you win. If not, you are dead. But you started dead – so what the heck.

As Erica Jung put it, "if you don't risk anything, you risk even more."

Chapter Ten

Shift Into High Gear

The market was down, clients were fuming and the managers and Advisors in the room were hurting. Yet the banner across the front of the meeting room proclaimed: "Shift Into High Gear".

"Are they nuts? Did they cut the budget so much they had to use a banner from a meeting in 1999?" "Just another clumsy attempt by our out-of-touch senior management to drive production any way they can." "Don't the fools know that you shift into a lower gear when you are driving a car up a hill—and we are climbing a mountain."

The metaphor did make sense because it was not about a car. Rather, the analogy referred to a mode of transportation that gives a lot more self-determination to the rider: a bicycle.

When riding up a long, steep mountain, bicycle racers do shift into lower gears. But they don't stay there. Before they reach the top, the best riders start attacking the mountain. They shift into a higher gear, pop out of their saddle and pedal like mad. Often, it makes the difference between winning and losing the race.

There are three reasons this strategy works and all of them have parallels to advising and investing.

The first reason is mathematical. Assume a long hill has slowed the competitors to just 10 miles per hour. A rider who can pick up just 2 miles per hour will be riding 20% faster than her competition. If the same rider were to pick up 2 miles per hour when headed downhill at say 40 miles per hour, the increase is only 5%.

The next reason is physiological. Uphill is hard on everyone, but the rider who picks up a lead on the uphill can relax a little and recover on the downhill. The rider who is behind has to keep pedaling hard.

The last reason is psychological. After reaching the top of the hill the rider in front will be able to start zooming down the hill, thereby opening a substantial lead. In a sense it is a false lead. After all, the riders behind will also benefit from the momentum the downhill provides. Yet, upon reaching the top of the hill and seeing how far ahead the leader is, the riders behind suffer a psychological blow that further enhances the leader's advantage.

The point is simple: just as market timers have to jump back in before the market goes up, Advisors have to throw their energy back in before it gets easy. The time to shift into high gear is when it doesn't feel like it's time. It will give you the mathematical advantage of buying low, the physiological advantage of being able to coast a little and enjoy the good times when they return, and a psychological advantage on your competitors.

So irrespective of market conditions, ignore the personal pain and problems, get out of your saddle and pump hard for the peak.

Sources, Contributors and Influences

Faigie Richman
Bettina Herbert, M.D.
Alanna, Jason and Ryan Richman
Anita Alexander
Ron Arden
Andreas Calianos
Lisa Casden
Barron Clancy
Annie Cooke
John Coyne
Alison DeGrassi
Woody Dorsey
Rick Ezell
Mary Fleishmann
Dick Friedland
Ron Funk
Charlie Grose
Richard Grund
David Ix
Harris Lawless
David Leach M.D.
Bruce McClaren

Bill McIntosh
Tim Marinec
Ross Mayer
Barbara Munson
Stephen Roulac
Rabbi James Rosen
Richard Sumberg
Robert White
Chuck Widger
Dick Wollack
and especially Nan Spires without whom this book would never have happened.

Influences Books and Periodicals

Against the Gods Peter L. Bernstein,
The Age of Unreason Charles Handy
Barbarians to Bureaucrats Lawrence M. Miller
Change Watzlawick, Weakland and Fisch.
"The Economist Magazine" (17 years worth)
The End of History and the Last Man Francis Fukuyama
Extraordinary Popular Delusions and the Madness of Crowds
    Charles McKay, et al
Famous Financial Fiascos John Train
Genius James Gleick
A History of Knowledge Charles Van Doren
Innovator's Dilemma Clayton Christensen
It's Not About the Bike Lance Armstrong

A Mathematician Reads the Newspaper John Allen Paulos
The Meaning of It All Richard Feynman
Modern Times Paul Johnson
The Pleasure of Finding Things Out Richard Feynman
The Printing Revolution in Early Modern Europe Elizabeth
   Eisenstein
The Structure of Scientific Revolutions Thomas S. Kuhn
Thinking About Management Ted Levitt
The Western Tradition Eugene Weber
What You Can Change What You Can't Change Martin E. P.
   Seligman
Everything by Peter Drucker